DISCARD

DISSENTIENT VOICE

University of Notre Dame
Ward-Phillips Lectures in
English Language and Literature

Volume 11

DISSENTIENT VOICE

The Ward-Phillips Lectures
for 1980
with some Related Pieces

DONALD DAVIE

UNIVERSITY OF NOTRE DAME PRESS
NOTRE DAME • LONDON

Library of Congress Cataloging in Publication Data

Davie, Donald.
Dissentient voice.

(Ward-Phillips lectures in English language and literature; v. 11)
Includes index.
1. Christian poetry, English — History and criticism — Addresses, essays, lectures.
2. Dissenters, Religious — England — Addresses, essays, lectures. I. Title. II. Series.
PR508.C65D38   821'.009'382   81 — 40455
ISBN 0 — 268 — 00852 — 3   AACR2

Manufactured in the United States of America

Contents

Preface

When the University of Notre Dame honored me with an invitation
to deliver the Ward-Phillips lectures for 1980, I found that I wanted to
attempt a sort of sequel to the Clark lectures that I had given in
Cambridge in 1976, which were subsequently published as *A Gathered
Church* (1978). What sort of sequel should it be, however? On the one
hand I could have tied up some of the loose ends left hanging in *A
Gathered Church* — of which there were plenty, as my reviewers had
pointed out. On the other hand I could have tried to do what I
portentously threatened in the last of those lectures — "to challenge
certain received notions about the social and political history of
English Dissent over the past three centuries." In the event I did
neither; instead I have covered the same ground as in the Clark
lectures, using different examples. In particular, since *A Gathered
Church* strayed from the promise of its subtitle, "The Literature of the
English Dissenting Interest, 1700— 1930," I have sought to take my
examples more exclusively from literature narrowly considered,
indeed from poetry.

This means however that the historical scope of my enquiry is
even more presumptuous in the four lectures at Notre Dame than in
the six at Cambridge: two and a half centuries, more rather than less.
Not all the reviewers of *A Gathered Church* were sure that I was aware
of my presumption in attempting a survey so sweeping. I assure them
that I was, and am. English Nonconformity in the eighteenth century
is by itself a broad and fascinating field of historical enquiry, and I am
under no illusions that my grasp of the relevant evidence can begin to
match that of a specialist in this field, such as Geoffrey F. Nuttall.
Similarly, now that I have taken up the challenge of certain reviewers
(notably Daniel Jenkins) in trying to assess Robert Browning's place

in the historical perspective of English Dissent, I am well aware that specialists in Browning Studies will find my treatment of their poet altogether too bold and sketchy. But since my concern is precisely with the long historical perspective, not with any one moment or phase within that perspective, I hope it may be agreed that some painting in bold strokes is inevitable, and may be condoned. I have tried to make some slight amends by including, among the pieces which I have here appended to the Ward-Phillips lectures, one or two which take a narrower focus — on the period roughly 1770 – 1800.

I am afraid that my focusing on this span of years will aggravate the offence that I already gave, in *A Gathered Church*, to Unitarians. I am sorry about this, and must ask Unitarian readers to recognize that my enquiry is strictly historical; and that uncovering what I cannot help but see as successful duplicity in the early years of English Unitarianism is not meant to impugn the sincerity and high-mindedness of professing Unitarians at the present day.

This book, like *A Gathered Church,* is undeniably polemical. But those reviewers are wrong who thought, and doubtless will think, that the polemic is in the service of some prejudice political or religious. In my own sense of the matter, the polemic serves no other purpose than to impel us to use certain terms, certain English *words,* strictly and with scruple; to make us aware for instance of what we are doing when we extend the words "Christian" or "Dissenter" to comprehend people who deny both Original Sin and the Holy Trinity. Words have meanings, which can be defined; if a word is used in a way that the definition gives no warrant for, one may legitimately protest — not in order to be exclusive, but in order to be precise. In short, I am not aware of "carrying a torch" for English Nonconformity or for anything else — only for the English language which, like any other writer in that language, I have an interest in keeping crisp, supple, and responsible.

Daniel Jenkins and other reviewers of *A Gathered Church* protested that in my sourness about what English Nonconformity became in the nineteenth century I overlook what they propose as the socio-political achievements of that Nonconformity. The Nonconformist churches, said Mr. Jenkins, "had also to help new social groups to claim their rights"; and "Dissenters helped to lay the foundations of modern welfare society and to transform the Empire into the Commonwealth." Well, perhaps so. But my concern was, and is, with our language — with that language when used with most scruple and power, in our poetry. And what has this to do with "new social groups" claiming "their rights" — unless one were to ask, in an enquiry which would be quite different from mine, what is meant in this formulation by "new," by "social group," and by "rights"? A concern with what is called "social justice" may be nobler than what has impelled me; it is at all events quite different.

I am grateful to all those who reviewed *A Gathered Church,* not least those who were most hostile. I have tried to profit from their observations. And I am grateful to the University of Notre Dame, particularly to Professors Tom Werge and John Matthias, for supplying the incentive without which I would not have thought through again my perceptions about English Dissent. To these two, and to others in South Bend, I am moreover indebted for hearty hospitality and flattering attentions. Finally I thank the editors of *PN Review,* *Sewanee Review,* and *Proteus* for permission to reprint essays which first appeared in their pages.

Enlightenment and Christian Dissent

The Ward-Phillips Lectures
for 1980

LECTURE ONE

Poetry and the
English Enlightenment

There is a trap or a trick — at all events, a problem — in the title I have given to this lecture. For what was "the English Enlightenment"? "The Enlightenment" is a category of intellectual history which all of us Anglicists make play with from time to time (though significantly less often than our colleagues in French, in German, and in other languages); but I'm not aware of any book in English that we can point to, which defines "the English Enlightenment" in a way that commands general assent. The Americans indeed are not so culpable in this respect as the English; for "the American Enlightenment" has been vigorously discussed and argued about by students of American history, as the English Enlightenment hasn't been. At least one distinguished American historian, Daniel J. Boorstin, has been at pains to argue that there never was any such thing as an American Enlightenment, or else that if there was the Founders of the Republic had no part in it; but Mr. Boorstin I think is in a minority, and the consensus is that there was indeed an American Enlightenment, and that the Declaration of Independence and the Constitution of the United States are "Enlightenment" documents. Henry F. May's admirably thorough book of 1976, *The Enlightenment in America*, detects not one such American Enlightenment, but no less than *four*, to each of which he's prepared to assign dates; thus — "The Moderate Enlightenment," 1688 – 1787, "The Skeptical Enlightenment," 1750 – 1789, "The Revolutionary Enlightenment," 1776 – 1800, and "The Didactic Enlightenment," 1800 – 1815. And Garry Wills's *Inventing America* (1978) was concerned with arguing closely that Mr. Jefferson's Declaration of Independence derived from the Scottish Enlightenment rather than, as had been thought, from the English thinker John Locke. For yes, there was certainly a *Scottish* Enlightenment, as all of us — Scotsmen and others — are ready to agree; just as there was also by common consent a German Enlightenment, a Russian Enlightenment, a Latin American Enlightenment, and so on, not to speak of an Enlightenment in France where indeed, so many commentators would persuade us, the whole thing began or was concocted. But England, it seems, is the odd one out; for whereas few students of English history explicitly *deny* that the English participated in what was clearly an international movement in the spirit of Western man comparable to what we call two or three centuries earlier, "the Renaissance," yet among students of English history, whether English or not, the term is rather seldom used and, when it is used (as in Bertrand Bronson's *Facets of the Enlightenment* [1968]), it seems to be no more than a sonorous substitute for "the Eighteenth Century." Henry F. May's dates, ranging from the seventeenth century into the nineteenth, suggest that this at all events won't do; indeed, as soon as we turn to studies of the Enlightenment as an international phenomenon, we find it hard to deny that "the Enlightenment" must encompass Percy Bysshe Shelley in the 1820s, as well as the Englishmen Bacon and Thomas Hobbes in the seventeenth century, not to speak of the Italian Nicolo Macchiavelli in the sixteenth.

All this, it will be seen, puts me in a quandary. Plainly what we have to do with, in this dubiety about an English Enlightenment — was there such a thing? if so when did it happen? how do we define it? — is a redoubtable problem in intellectual history, for the solution of which I would need all of these four lectures, if not indeed many more. And yet what I need, for the quite different investigation that I have in mind, is a working agreement between you and me (not a working *definition*, but rather no more than a shared sense) of what we may take the English Enlightenment to be.

In these circumstances I have no alternative but to be bold — which is to say, impressionistic and personal. And to get the worst impudence over to start with, I offer, to explain some of what *I* mean by the English Enlightenment, a poem of my own which I call "In the Geography School":

> Fire-drives of Folsom man!
> Around the university's

Degree-giving occasion
The stubble burns in Essex.

The great savannahs are
The products of our fires,
All natural resources
Were cultural appraisals

Once. The scarlet doctors
Hark to an Asian age
Of the earliest cultivations
By arms of the China Sea:

Turmeric, and for saffron
The autumnal crocus, plantings
For pigments, not for food
But dyes to fix their stations.

The imagination holds
In the Old World's promontory, Europe,
Not by the hues of degree.
It is launched on the *llanos,* the wolds;

And as upon nothing scorched,
No impoverished assemblage,
Ash-groves burnt off, but as
Through an organic household.

Seas. Of grass.
The haze of Indian Summer
Smells of smoke. The Chancellor
And the Vice-Chancellor pass,

The Doctors, the Honorary Fellow,
And the Bachelors of Arts.
A reader in the Library
Whispers, "Venezuela!"

This poem, I must explain, was written some fifteen years ago, during the period (1964– 68) when I was associated with a then new university in England, the University of Essex; and it reflects something of what in my head as I and my colleagues struggled to set up what it is convenient, though not quite accurate, to describe as a Department of Comparative Literature.

By decisions taken before any of us were appointed, we students of literature and our close associates in the department of

Government — along with later some mostly half-hearted sociologists and economists and art-historians — were required to pay particular attention, first, to British experience through the centuries, but secondly, and in parallel, to the historic experience of three regions of the earth's surface: North America, European and Asiatic Russia, and Latin America. Now, as soon as we began to ponder these three regions as cradles of human culture, we were forced to draw some conclusions of a practical sort. The first was very unwelcome and disconcerting: it was that for all practical purposes (since an *undergraduate* curriculum was what we were concerned with) the cultural histories of these three regions began in the second half of the eighteenth century; and it seemed to follow that our studies of English literature, if they were to keep meaningfully in step with study of one of these foreign literatures (and it was clear to us that they should), would have to be disproportionately weighted towards literature of the last 250 years. Thus a very painful sacrifice — of our earlier literature — was exacted from us at the start. On the other hand, I thought, could we not turn this very disadvantage to good account by giving particular attention (as we could hardly avoid doing anyway) to the category or phase of cultural history that goes by the name of "the Enlightenment" (*die aufklärung, le siècle des lumières*)? Indeed, was it not just here that I and Jean Blondel, the Professor of Government, could begin to meet another of the obligations that had been wished upon us — of breaking down some of the fences customarily erected between the so-called Social Sciences and the so-called Arts? For those social or behavioral sciences — Economics, Political Science, Sociology, along with others that in truth attracted me more, like Anthropology and Cultural Geography — by common consent emerged, in anything like their modern form, out of the climate of ideas that we call (whatever we mean by it) "the Enlightenment." And so it seemed that our freshmen could and should, at one and the same time, be given a grounding in eighteenth-century history and be forced into a critical scrutiny of one or another scholarly discipline, introduced indeed to the philosophical problem of just what "discipline" in this sense means.

But here we ran up against a comically rudimentary difficulty: our university had decided that it could manage without any historians at all! This is hard to believe, but so it was. Of course it has been put right since, but how could the philistine error have arisen in the first place? Only, I think, because both then and since the fashionableness in many fields of what is called "structuralist" has masked a profound and widespread impatience with the recorded past, simply with the extent and the copiousness of it; and a determination that its awkwardly circumstantial records should in future, so far as possible, gather dust unread. Fortunately Blondel and I had too much respect for the traditional educations we had received — he in France, and I in England — for us to plot our joint curriculum in such structuralist terms. As Jean would say, using a Gallicism that delighted me: "But that, you know — it is not *amusing*!" So after much difficulty we got the historians we demanded, so that our students should not learn about for instance "colonialism" without learning also, and more, about colonies and colonists; so that they should not be nourished on more or less neatly matching paradigms and diagrams, but on disparities, particularities, *quiddities*.

And yet this too of course has its dangers. It is all very well and necessary to puncture the presumption of the rationalist, abstracting into diagrams; but on the other hand one mustn't detract from the dignity of the human Reason, by denying that it can responsibly generalize (and *abstract*) from an array of particular cases. Indeed just here, I venture to think, is one urgently persistent problem that "the Enlightenment" presents us with: in the distinctions that have to be made between the rational and the reasonable, or else between rationalism and rationality. These are the distinctions that the Age of Reason, and its poets, were struggling to make, and they failed, for our intellectual and imaginative life is still maimed by the lack of them — as this excursus into a chapter of my professional past is meant to show. Patriotism, most people would agree, is eminently *reasonable* but a rationalist can show it isn't *rational*. Because we are still mired in these dilemmas, our eighteenth-century ancestors who struggled in the same morass cannot help but be very near to us.

They are near to us in other ways, much nearer I believe than their nineteenth-century successors. How this may be, we see if I remind you of the three foreign areas we at Essex were to take particular note of. North America, South America, Russia — what they have in common is something so blindingly obvious that it can be overlooked: all three name landmasses of continental scale, and by virtue of that in the starkest contrast to what we at Essex had to relate them to — the area of the British Isles, by comparison so exiguous. Accordingly, should not our Essex students first take the measure, physically, of Russia and the Americas; and recognize, then and there, just how *small* the home islands are — how restricted the distances, the range of different terrains and weathers, and conceivably therefore of psychological states, or at least of natural images for such states? Certainly something so massively rudimentary as that was part of what I imagined in the mind of the student in my poem, when he whispered "Venezuela!" If that student should also wonder at the number and stature of the cultural monuments that the small islands have produced, by comparison with the continents, that would be another factor in a developing equation that we might call "proportion," and might even name as "civilization," as "education."

There is a magnificent moment in our eighteenth-century poetry where there is registered just this explosive enlargement of an insular or European sense of scale into a scale that is on the contrary continental or oceanic. It uses, it so happens, just that unEnglish word "savannah" that I made play with in my poem. And it occurs in the second book of Thomson's *Seasons,* where Thomson has pondered what summer must be like in the torrid zone. After an account of tropical fruits, Thomson is suddenly overawed:

> From these the prospect varies. Plains immense
> Lie stretched below, interminable meads
> And vast savannas, where the wandering eye,
> Unfixt, is in a verdant ocean lost.

It is too bad that I cannot go on quoting what is a magnificently composed and consciously ambiguous passage of blank verse. But these four lines sufficiently make the point, which is brought out and discussed very sensitively indeed by Mr. John Barrell in his book about Thomson and John Clare, *The Idea of Landscape and the Sense of Place, 1730 – 1840.* Thomson, indolent and stay-at-home in his life but admirably meticulous and exacting in his art, and venturesome in his imagination, had mastered for the sake of his art the laws of composition that for the sake of *his* art the painter Claude Lorraine had mastered — a way of ordering, and thus *mastering*, whatever landscapes western Europe might present; but faced in imaginative reading with the wholly different non-European landscapes of the savannah, Thomson concedes (wherein his greatness, surely) that the Claudian glass won't serve — the eye is "wandering," is "unfixt," is "lost," it knows no way to *command* a prospect so different from those it has been trained on. And of course this happens elsewhere in *The Seasons;* exuberantly excited by the new continental vistas that Whig maritime and commercial imperialism had opened up for the British imagination, Thomson time and again ascends to a height from which (quite as if he had known what it is like to travel in a jet aircraft) he can look down and, in a perspective undreamed of by Claude Lorraine, see for instance the Orinoco river emptying out into the ocean and staining its blue waters brown. The *shock* of that sudden alteration of scale is caught by Thomson and a few other eighteenth-century poets as it could not be by Victorian poets to whom the imperial vistas were more commonplace.

In thinking along these lines, I was rather keenly aware how I had been myself affected by a sojourn in the western United States, and more remotely by another, twenty-four years earlier, in Arctic Russia — to which was added, while I was at Essex, an altogether more scurrying and less satisfactory visit to South America. What I had experienced, particularly in California and Nevada and Utah, was something astringent and liberating: a wholly non-European sense of how in forbidding and sparsely peopled landscapes the human being has no special privileged status, but must compete for living room and security with nonhuman creatures like scorpions and bodies of water. The proportion that I had taken for granted, between the human and the nonhuman creation, was knocked from under me. And this was frightening, but the fright was salutary; the human race's purchase on the earth's surface and the earth's resources was more precarious than Western Europe was aware of. For the registering of that fright, that *horror* (for the emotion was as intense as that), I find that once again I have to go to the eighteenth century — to Goldsmith, in *The Traveller*:

> Where wild Oswego spreads her swamps around,
> And Niagara stuns with thundering sound . . .

This, as everyone knows, was elaborated into a famous passage near the end of *The Deserted Village,* about the scenes which attend the expropriated villagers on the other side of the ocean:

> Those poisonous fields with rank luxuriance crowned,
> Where the dark scorpion gathers death around;
> Where at each step the stranger fears to wake
> The rattling terrors of the vengeful snake;
> Where crouching tigers wait their hapless prey,
> And savage men more murderous still than they;
> While oft in whirls the mad tornado flies,
> Mingling the ravaged landscape with the skies.

We are accustomed to snigger at Goldsmith's ignorance of the actual fauna and flora of the state of Georgia, or else with haughty erudition to rebut such misreading by pointing out for instance that Goldsmith, following Buffon, meant by "tiger" some dozen carnivores, including the cougar. But we would be better employed, much of the time, acknowledging how Goldsmith here articulates the inescapable and natural response of the western European confronting the lethal extremity and luxuriance of the Southern States, even today.

What I had discovered those years ago, and now try to articulate (as I tried in Essex), is the abiding relevance and imaginative richness of Geography, that subject which through school and university I had always thought of as a plodding and fusty occupation for second-rate minds content with memorizing accurately and drawing neatly. What enlightened me — and of course I say "enlightened" advisedly — was, first, non-European landscapes themselves, but secondly a poet: the six-foot-something Swedish-American Charles Olson, who began his "Maximus to Gloucester, Letter 27" with:

> I come back to the geography of it . . .

and who ended that poem:

> that forever the geography
> which leans in
> on me I compell

backwards I compell Gloucester
to yield, to
change
    Polis
is this

In Olson's pamphlet, *A Bibliography on America for Ed Dorn* (such texts
were in those years available in London and Cambridge — not any
more), I read of, and duly noted and followed up, names like Walter
Prescott Webb, the historian of the American frontier; and one
Anderson, practitioner of an enlightened and undreamed-of discipline called, I suppose, "palaeo-botany" or "the history of agricul-
ture." Above all I encountered the name of the great modern
geographer Carl Sauer. And all of the matters canvassed in my
poem — that many if not all of the great grasslands of the world were
created artificially in prehistory, by primitive hunters using fire to
round up and drive the beasts they had to kill; or the possibility that
some plants were first cultivated in prehistory not for food but for
dyestuffs — came to me first out of Sauer's writings. They intrigued
me when I first encountered them, and I sought to promote them
enthusiastically in my poem, not as demonstrated or demonstrable
truths but on the contrary precisely as "intriguing" — as learned
speculations which could stimulate and release the imagination into
looking down undreamed-of perspectives on human history, a history to be read less out of old records than out of landscapes. Years
later in California I met Sauer — a sprightly, lean, physically dried-
out octogenarian, every inch a Midwesterner and a living link (so I
apprehended him) with the immigrant pioneering generations of the
great grassland states. He knew, when I asked him, that his work had
interested poets; Olson in particular he recalled, "the big Swede" as
he called him, but it was in an inattentively amused tone that he spoke
of him, almost impatiently, certainly with condescension. Though he
had as a young man fought his own battles with what he called
"positivism," and had even in passing praised poets' apprehensions of
"the areal" (that last very much one of his words, which accordingly,
through Olson, finds its way into Edward Dorn's poetry), still Sauer
was enough a man of his time and generation to be rather proudly a

scientist, interested as he thought only in the ultimately demonstrable, and so committed to dismissing poetry as, in the end or sooner,
less than serious. I don't think we know whether the great cultural
geographer Montesquieu took a more generous line to the poets
whom he stimulated, like Thomas Gray and Goldsmith, than Sauer
took towards Olson and Dorn.

At any rate, however it might be with my associates and allies at
Essex, I made a new connection here with "the Enlightenment." For
if I asked myself what poems in English, before those that Olson and
Dorn and I were writing, had last gone for imaginative sustenance
to geography on an oceanic and continental and millenial scale, I
found myself naming those classics of the English Enlightenment:
Goldsmith's *The Traveller,* Gray's *Education & Government,* Thomson's
The Seasons; though also Coleridge's *Ancient Mariner* and some poems
by that youthful Wordsworth who, at home in Westmorland, knew
the family of Fletcher Christian, leader of the mutineers of the *Bounty,*
those who sailed to and populated Pitcairn Island. It was later, after I
had left Essex for California, that I came to see how this aspect of the
Enlightenment, not its rationalistic arrogance but on the contrary its
humbled awe before the revealed plenitude of human terrains and
human cultures, was inscribed — as on language by Gray and Montesquieu, Thomson and Goldsmith — so on the maps and charts of
the world by Cook and George Vancouver, La Pérouse and La
Vérendrye, Abel Tasman and Vitus Behring. It was the discovery of
Melanesian and Polynesian cultures by the great Enlightenment
navigators like Cook and Bligh, Bougainville, and the American John
Ledyard (this last read by me, on the prompting of an Edward Dorn
poem, inside blizzard-stormed tin walls in Iowa in 1965), which
finally exploded, for thoughtful and responsible people in Western
Europe, the assumption that cultural and moral and civic standards
had been established once and for all, at the start of the Christian era,
by three mediterranean cultures: Greek, and Roman, and Hebrew. In
strictly literary histories I am apprised of nothing which can explain,
so comprehensively as this does, why at the end of the eighteenth
century a classical or neoclassical culture gave way to a culture that
we have to call, however uneasily, "romantic." The cultural *relativism*
that these discoveries induced is famously pinpointed in Diderot's

reflections on Tahitian society in his *Supplément à Bougainville*. But Diderot's tendentiously simplified polemic, notoriously a founding document of that great nonsense "the noble savage," is humanly surpassed by a passage of English poetry when Cowper, in Book I of *The Task*, broods on the fate and feelings of Omai, the South Sea Islander returned to his native shores after being the fashionable toast of a London season:

> But far beyond the rest, and with most cause,
> Thee, gentle savage! whom no love of thee
> Or thine, but curiosity, perhaps,
> Or else vain-glory, prompted us to draw
> Forth from thy native bowers, to show thee here
> With what superior skill we can abuse
> The gifts of Providence, and squander life.
> The dream is past; and thou hast found again
> Thy cocoas and bananas, palms and yams,
> And homestall thatched with leaves. But hast thou found
> Their former charms? And having seen our state,
> Our palaces, our ladies, and our pomp
> Of equipage, our gardens, and our sports,
> And heard our music; are thy simple friends,
> Thy simple fare, and all thy plain delights
> As dear to thee as once? And have thy joys
> Lost nothing by comparison with ours?
> Rude as thou art (for we returned thee rude
> And ignorant, except of outward show),
> I cannot think thee yet so dull of heart
> And spiritless, as never to regret
> Sweets tasted here, and left as soon as known.
> Methinks I see thee straying on the beach,
> And asking of the surge that bathes thy foot
> If ever it has washed our distant shore.
> I see thee weep, and thine are honest tears,
> A patriot's for his country: thou art sad
> At thought of her forlorn and abject state,
> From which no power of thine can raise her up.
> Thus fancy paints thee, and, though apt to err,
> Perhaps errs little when she paints thee thus.
> She tells me too, that duly every morn
> Thou climb'st the mountain top, with eager eye

Exploring far and wide the watery waste
For sight of ship from England. Every speck
Seen in the dim horizon turns thee pale
With conflict of contending hopes and fears.
But comes at last the dull and dusky eve,
And sends thee to thy cabin, well prepared
To dream all night of what the day denied.
Alas! expect it not. We found no bait
To tempt us in thy country. Doing good,
Disinterested good, is not our trade.
We travel far, 'tis true, but not for naught;
And must be bribed to compass earth again
By other hopes and richer fruits than yours.

The texture of this blank verse is lax and prosy, as for the most part
Thomson's isn't. But if we attend to the sentiments expressed, have
we gone beyond them in our attitudes towards what we have been
taught to call "the Third World"? It seems to me we haven't, and that
for instance fifteen years ago when Ed Dorn, in a collection prog-
rammatically entitled *Geography*, assailed Lyndon Johnson's U.S.A.
on behalf of the exploited poor of the Banana Republics, Dorn could
not move an inch further than Cowper's caustic shame on behalf of
Omai. Instead of Diderot's facile opposition between innocent and
noble *them*, and hypocritically ignoble *us*, Cowper confronts what we
all now realize as the really intractable consequence of European
imperialism: a sort of people like Omai, who are no longer either
"them" or "us," but betwixt-and-between, at home in neither culture
but stranded between them.

Here, though, we reach another difficulty in our understanding of
what we mean by "the Enlightenment." I have called *The Seasons* and
Gray's *Education & Government* and *The Traveller* "classics of the English
Enlightenment"; can I say as much of *The Task*, written by a dogmatic
and evangelical Calvinist, whose Calvinism is openly expressed in his
poem? We may, and I fear do, suppose that Gray's Christianity, and
Thomson's, and Goldsmith's, were merely nominal and Erastian;
though the evidence is far to seek in all these cases, and in
Goldsmith's points clearly the opposite way. But the case of Cowper
cannot be huddled away in this fashion. And so the question arises
quite inescapably: may we suppose that "the Enlightenment" is

fundamentally, if not indeed by definition, an irreligious, an *anti*-religious phenomenon? Whether or not we *may* do this, there's no doubt that many of us do; particularly in Marxist circles, where "the Enlightenment" is commonly invoked as highly commendable, one reason for commending it is that it allegedly refused to smoke "the opium of the masses." And thus I have been reproved for wondering if John Wesley, who recommended Christianity as an eminently *reasonable* religion, could be regarded as a figure of the English Enlightenment. But once we begin to apply this standard, we soon find, not just that that devoutly agonized Anglican Samuel Johnson has to be expelled from "the Enlightenment," but that there is hardly one of our eighteenth-century poets who does not have to be cast likewise into obscurantist darkness. For there is not a one of them whose claims to a properly "enlightened" infidelity will stand up to inspection. (And what are we to do for instance with that uncomfortably fervent Christian, Christopher Smart?) Unless I am mistaken, we here confront a dilemma which has reverberations far outside the field of English poetry or even of English literature. On the one hand we may decide that "the Enlightenment" is indeed essentially an antireligious phenomenon, not just anticlerical but antireligious — in which case the English Enlightenment comprises only deists and those Unitarians of whom that excellent writer, our Marxist historian E. P. Thompson, has written that they "pushed God so far back into his Baconian heaven of first causes that he became, except for purposes of moral incantation, quite ineffectual"; *or else* we refuse an "Enlightenment" conceived too exclusively on the French model, and declare that there was indeed an English Enlightenment in which, as not in Papist France, Protestant Christianity played a very large, perhaps a directing, rôle. In the latter case — which is, as will be discerned, the alternative that I prefer — other alleged "Enlightenments" (the German, the Russian, the Latin American) may breathe a little more freely, being released from the Voltairean straitjacket; and certainly it is only on this understanding that we can save for "the Enlightenment" any English poet of greater stature than Soame Jenyns.

And if, with this understanding of our eighteenth century as a profoundly *Christian* century, we look for the continuing life of eighteenth century poetry in our own time, we shall not automatically exclude from consideration those poets of our time who write — tormentedly, for the most part — out of the Christian communion. We shall be ready to discern, for instance, a Swiftian and thereby Christian note of self-disgust — a recognizably dry eighteenth-century voice — in this poem, called "The End," by my English contemporary C. H. Sisson:

> I shall never hear the angelic choir
> Sing, as it assuredly does, I shall walk in hell
> Among tinkers and tailors and other riff-raff.
> Another damnation for imagining myself among those
> Whose fornications came as easy as winking
> And whose pilferings of other people
> Were a social bounty which did not stop at themselves.
> I knew early what there was to be known about me
> Only lacked courage, fortitude, élan
> And so descended into a consuming whirlpool
> Round and round, here I am at the last gurgle.

Where do we locate the antecedents of this plain and passionate asperity, and this driving colloquialism ("tinkers and tailors and other riff-raff"), if not in the eighteenth century of Jonathan Swift?

And yet here we need to pause. Hearing the tone of Swift, we are carried back into the eighteenth century, certainly. But is that the same as saying we are carried back to "the Enlightenment"? We have already warned ourselves not to use "the Enlightenment" and "the eighteenth century" as if they meant the same thing. And if as I have proposed we take the note of the English Enlightenment to be the delighted and awestruck excitement at new vistas and new horizons that we find in Thomson's *Seasons* (vistas and horizons, incidentally, in the mental as well as in the physical world — Thomson was an admirer of Isaac Newton), do we not have to say that this is specifically what we do *not* find in Swift? Much of the time Swift, like his friend Alexander Pope, is rather furiously tugging against, and resisting, just those commercial and scientific and imperialistic developments which so fired the imagination of James Thomson. Much of the time Swift and Pope are castigating their century for departing from the habits of the century before; they are rather consistently backward-looking, both of them. There *may* be texts of Swift which can properly be described as "of the Enlightenment," and in Pope there certainly are; but in both authors, as I read them, there are many more texts which are not. And so I am constrained to think that the distinction between "Enlightenment" and "non-Enlightenment," as I understand those terms, may have to be drawn inside a writer's *oeuvre*; we may judge him as "of the Enlightenment" at one point, but not at others.

And so there arises the possibility that for the religious poetry of the English Enlightenment we should look not to Swift but to a sector of the Christian communion in England which, as we know, he hated bitterly — to the Protestant Dissenters. Something like this, for instance, from the pen of Swift's contemporary, the great Independent (as we would say, Congregationalist) hymn-writer, Isaac Watts:

> Hosanna to the royal son
> Of David's ancient line!
> His natures two, his person one,
> Mysterious and divine.
>
> The root of David, here we find,
> And offspring, are the same:
> Eternity and time are joined
> In our Immanuel's name.
>
> Blest he that comes to wretched man
> With peaceful news from Heaven!
> Hosannas, of the highest strain,
> To Christ the Lord be given.
>
> Should we, dear Lord, refuse to take
> The Hosanna on our tongues,
> The rocks and stones would rise and break
> Their silence into songs.[1]

Neither C. H. Sisson nor any one else in our time writes poems like this. New hymns are composed for us, and at times we contrive to sing them in church without intolerable discomfort. But our serious poets, if they are Christian, write as Sisson does of their solitary and private religious *experience;* whereas Watts writes of and for the communal experience of worship, and so he deals not with self-disgusted desolations nor for that matter with feelingful exaltations, but with Christianity in its public form, as *doctrine*. These are hymns for theologians — because, in those far-off days, religious leaders like Watts were sanguine enough to think that the humblest worshipper could and should be enough of a theologian to understand the tenets of the Faith which he professed. Hence the sinewy intellectualism of this poem — the compressed wit which expresses the paradox of Jesus belonging at once to Eternity and to Time by saying that in him "The root of David . . . And offspring, are the same." This intellectualism, surely, is what makes such a poem at home in "the Age of Reason"; and Watts's sanguine confidence in the capacities of his fellow Dissenters, something which led him to compose for them schemes of self-education and treatises of logic as well as devotional tracts, is what ranges Watts along with a poet of the Enlightenment like Thomson. In the next generation as much can be claimed for at any rate some of the hymns of Charles Wesley.

In conclusion, however belatedly, I should like to vindicate these poets of the English Enlightenment on that score which, ever since Wordsworth's Preface to *Lyrical Ballads*, has been taken to be their weakest flank — that is to say, their poetic diction. My text shall be, once again, Goldsmith's *The Traveller*:

> To men of other minds my fancy flies,
> Embosomed in the deep where Holland lies.
> Methinks her patient sons before me stand,
> Where the broad ocean leans against the land,
> And, sedulous to stop the coming tide,
> Lift the tall rampire's artificial pride.
> Onward, methinks, and diligently slow,
> The firm-connected bulwark seems to grow;
> Spreads its long arms amidst the watery roar,
> Scoops out an empire and usurps the shore;
> While the pent ocean, rising o'er the pile,
> Sees an amphibious world beneath him smile:
> The slow canal, the yellow-blossomed vale,
> The willow-tufted bank, the gliding sail,
> The crowded mart, the cultivated plain,
> A new creation rescued from his reign.

"Where the broad ocean leans against the land . . ."! Goldsmith here, the agrarian and reactionary Tory, shows himself — unlike those earlier Tories, Pope and Swift — at one with Thomson the exuberant Whig. Goldsmith too could be looking down from a jet aircraft coming in over the Low Countries; and not just looking, but feeling in his own frame (by empathy, therefore — that term so woefully misused in our criticism to replace "sympathy") the elementary *dynamics* of sea encountering land: "leans," he says, "the broad ocean *leans* against the land." The perception embodied in that verb is a product of abstraction — such abstraction from detail as the jet pilot enjoys, looking down, or the geographer, poring over the physical map. And yet it is profoundly imaginative — the imagination works through the abstraction, and proceeds indeed *by abstraction.* You will see that we have in a fashion come full circle — on to the demands that the human Reason may and must legitimately make, as it goes about its business of abstracting and so generalizing, abstracting from the innumerable details of the physical world so as to contrive the art or science of Geography, or from the multifarious manifestations of the metaphysical world so as to practice the art or science of Theology. The facile opposition that our criticism has made so much play with — between the concrete and the abstract — is here seen for the *ignis fatuus* that it is. Though critics and poetic theorists may have been hung up on this sterile because unfounded antithesis, our good poets never were. Were there world enough and time, I could demonstrate this. For the moment . . . "Where the broad ocean leans against the land" — would that I had written such a line!

Note

1. Text from Toplady's *Psalms and Hymns for Public and Private Worship* (London, 1776). For justification for thus not taking the text of a hymn from its earliest chronological version, see *post* : "The Language of the Eighteenth-Century Hymn."

LECTURE TWO

Enlightenment & Dissent

In my first lecture I touched upon several features of what I am venturing to call "The English Enlightenment." And I do not want to forget, nor would I have you forget, any of these features. But I want to dwell on one of them in particular: on the point that in England, however it may have been in France, the Enlightenment was not necessarily, still less *essentially*, unchristian. Once we have seized the point that in the Enlightenment the poetic imagination could and did quite naturally work by way of *abstraction*, we perceive that it could hardly stop short of those awesomely abstract, because paradoxical, conceptions that are the matter of theology. Christopher Smart writes, at the end of his "Hymn for the Nativity of Our Lord and Saviour Jesus Christ":

> Spinks and ouzels sing sublimely
> 'We too have a Saviour born';
> Whiter blossoms burst untimely
> On the blest Mosaic thorn.
>
> God all-bounteous, all creative,
> Whom no ills from good dissuade,
> Is incarnate and a native
> Of the very world he made.

This poem as a whole is very insistently English, because it works — right through to these last stanzas — with the peculiarly English legend of the miraculous Glastonbury thorn, which blossoms only at Christmas, having been planted (so the legend goes) by Joseph of Arimathaea. But there is no way, out of English legend or English history or English landscape, to escape the extraordinarily strenuous conceptualizing that the last two lines demand of us, in order to understand that the same energy which created the entire universe has condescended to become a human baby and therefore "Is incarnate and a native/ Of the very world he made." Whether or not we in fact accept this, as an article of faith, is poetically as much beside the point as whether we endorse Oliver Goldsmith's Tory-agrarian diagnosis of what was wrong with England in the 1760s; in either case the leap — not of faith, but of imagination — is breathtaking. In either case the sheer conception is grand and elevating, therefore liberating — whether we conceive of how the ocean *leans* upon the land, or of how a Creator might incarnate himself and so become one of his own creatures. In both cases the evidence of our senses is not denied or contradicted but simply surpassed, leaped over. And so Smart's verses are, just like Goldsmith's, an achievement not indeed of rationalism but of rationality, an instance of just how far the human Reason can go in conceiving the unperceivable and the logically impossible.

And in the Wesleys — in John, but more pertinently in his poet-brother Charles, the hymn-writer — we encounter audacities, imaginative abstractings, that in the same way ought to leave us gasping (though apparently they don't):

> Him the angels all adored,
>   Their Maker and their King;
> Tidings of their humbled Lord
>   They now to mortals bring.
> Emptied of His majesty,
>   Of his dazzling glories shorn,
> Being's source begins to be,
>   And God Himself is born!

"Being's source begins to be . . .", "Is incarnate and a native/ Of the very world he made" . . . Is it not clear that in both cases (as it happens prompted by the same occasion, the Incarnation) the human intellect — not primarily the sympathies of the human heart, but the energies of human Reason — is stretched to the limit? Was this not also what we found in Isaac Watts's "Hosanna to Christ"? And is it not clear therefore that all these are entirely appropriate manifestations of what we still laxly call (without attending to what we are saying) the Age of Reason?

Moreover, what are those "dazzling glories" of which, in Charles Wesley's poem, God is "shorn" when he condescends to be incarnate, those glories to which after the Crucifixion he returns? What are they but light, "the Uncreated Light," according to a tradition which reaches back through Dante's *Paradiso* to Scripture itself? *Light* — this is "Enlightenment"! So how did Unbelievers have the presumption to make of this ancient metaphor *their* peculiar property? And how is it that Believers were and are ready to acquiesce in the impudent takeover? Who says, or who ever proved or could prove, that the light which breaks — on the eighteenth or any other century — is by definition a secular light, not the light of a Divine Intelligence mediated to us through Grace? It is the merest arrogant prejudice that, flying in the face of what we know biographically about Christopher Smart and Charles Wesley, both eager students of the most advanced thought of their time, would deny that they were men of the Enlightenment and their poems products of the Enlightenment.

This prejudice, because it has gone unchallenged for so long, is now very confident. Thus E. P. Thompson, whom I cited in my first lecture, can assure his fellow-Marxists that "the eighteenth-century Church can scarcely be said to have had an articulated ideology." And he can be sure, apparently, that no one of his readers will ask: "What about Christopher Smart and Samuel Johnson, Joseph Butler or George Berkeley or William Law?" Not an articulated ideology among the lot of them, it seems! The same historian can assure us that "Wesleyanism . . . was self-consciously *anti*-Enlightenment"; and can go on to explain that he says this "not in any pejorative sense, but in the sense that the Wesleys turned their backs upon certain polite and rational modes, and reemphasized the paternalized responsibilities of the Church for the unenlightened majority."[1] That the mode of the Wesleyan hymns was not always "polite" I will concede; on the other hand I have just contended that the mode of at any rate Charles Wesley's hymns was insistently and vehemently "rational," unless we give to "rational" an unacceptably restricted sense. And as for "the paternalized responsibilities of the Church for the unenlightened majority," this seems to mean only that Wesleyan pastors were frequently as solicitous for the worldly welfare of their flocks as were conscientious pastors in the Anglican, the Roman, and the Dissenting communions (though what it really means, I suspect, is that at the time of the American Revolution both the Wesleys were vehement loyalists).

In case you are wondering, I stand before you not as a Methodist (which I am not) nor as a champion of the Wesley brothers (great and pious men though I believe they were, both of them). I take up the cudgels for Wesleyanism only because the prejudice against it is the particular instance that seems to lie across my path as I try to understand what we do mean, and what we might mean, when we talk, in the cultural history of England, of "the Enlightenment." It so happens, in fact, that my principal concern is with a quite different body of Christian believers, whom I have just invoked by speaking of "the Dissenting communions." Those heirs to the Cromwellian puritans — the Baptists, the Independents (Congregationalists, as they later called themselves), the Quakers, the English as distinct from the Scottish Presbyterians — what happened to them in the eighteenth century? It is after all rather astonishing how little we hear of them, quite suddenly, once we pass the date 1700 in any survey of English history. They have been taken note of, however, particularly by some of our Marxist colleagues, who thereby deserve the gratitude not just of Free Churchmen but of anyone who aspires to the unattainable ideal of disinterested enquiry. E. P. Thompson for instance, who is certainly one of that minority of Marxists who have earned our gratitude on these grounds, is harsh to the Wesleyans only so as to pay a compliment to what he calls "Old Dissent." This appears in his vastly influential work, *The Making of the English Working Class* (1964). Elsewhere he has declared: "The historian of ideas must see Old Dissent, with its strong intellectual traditions and its mercantile and professional support, as serving increasingly, after 1750, as a vector of the Enlightenment."[2] Sectarian infighting is a bore, and must be resisted. The important question here is very obvious, and can be posed quite simply: if the Enlightenment is to be understood as a triumph of the secular, infidel intelligence, then how can there be enlisted in its service a body of opinion and sentiment which is explicitly *Christian:* that heterogenous body of Christian belief which, because of developments peculiar to Anglo-American history, gets itself called "Dissent"? The answer is that in Marxist and more generally "liberal" ideology it is taken for granted that the complex of beliefs called for instance "Baptist" is only an untenable way-stage on the journey from unenlightened Belief to enlightened Unbelief. If I refuse to accept this, one reason is that both my parents — strongly "intellectual" indeed, but neither "mercantile" nor "professional" — went to their graves supposing that the Baptist Christianity which they professed was no halfway house but a coherent and consistent system of belief; in short, I suppose, an "articulated ideology." I am not prepared to give up my inheritance without a fight; and whereas I have no wish to make converts to their persuasion (which, as it happens, I no longer adhere to myself), nevertheless I won't see their convictions casually laughed out of court, nor smilingly condescended to as an acceptable stage on the way to something more laudable, more "enlightened." The acme of Enlightenment on *that* showing is the vehement and explicit anti-Christian, Tom Paine; and sure enough we have seen Tom Paine claimed for Dissent, called "a Dissenter," for no better reason than that one of his parents was a member of the Society of Friends!

However, let us be grateful. Old Dissent must be seen "as serving . . . as a vector of the Enlightenment." Yes, indeed — the point is an important one, and it is very seldom made, least of all by those supposed heirs of Old Dissent, the "Free Churchmen" or "nonconformists" of our own day. The Baptists for instance of the 1760s and 1770s, whether in the home islands or in the colonies, seem to have been quite often "enlightened," both in the general sense of that term and even in terms of that time-bounded climate of ideas which we call (when we think about it) *the* Enlightenment. They were very different creatures from the philistine fundamentalists of a later age in the Bible Belt, or in South London and the depressed areas of English industrial cities. Take for an example Isaac Backus of Connecticut, leader of the American Baptists at the Continental Congress and a contumacious thorn in the side of the state church of Massachusetts. Backus was a devoted admirer of that sage of the Enlightenment, John Locke; and he consistently refused to give up to unbelievers the metaphor of "enlightenment," of light breaking — as when, in his *Appeal to the Public for Religious Liberty,* he asserted that, whereas "the state is armed with the *sword* to guard the peace, and the civil rights of all persons and societies, and to punish those who violate the same," on the other hand "the church is armed with *light and truth,* to pull down the strongholds of iniquity, and to gain souls to Christ, and into his Church . . ."³ "The church is armed with *light* . . ."! Backus believed that Lockean Reason and scriptural Revelation pointed the same way; but that certainly didn't mean that he denied the authority of Revelation, or was blind to the light that broke from it. And the same is true of his fellow-sectaries on the other side of the ocean, whether they took the part of the American colonists (as many of them did), or loyally supported King George (as rather more of them did than it is now convenient to remember).

How and when and why, in the succeeding century, the dissenting churches became predominantly *un*enlightened is a story that no one seems to have told, doubtless because no one would get any thanks for telling it. Undoubtedly, though for many decades after the Revolution the British and the American dissenting churches worked closely together (for instance in the institution of the first foreign missions — to India and Burma), the American story and the British story are quite distinct. About the British story, I have a few ideas; as regards the American story I know only enough to marvel that so few of us, American or British, know even a little (and cannot easily determine where to go to learn more). Of Isaac Backus, who survived as a staunch Jeffersonian until 1806, William G. McLoughlin has decided: "it would be erroneous to portray Backus as a man of the Enlightenment in any profound sense. He was not really interested in science and his preoccupation with the reality and direct manifestations of divinity in revivals and conversions predisposed him to favor supernatural explanations for peculiar events."⁴ With this we must agree. But it remains true that the evangelical Christianity which Backus represents was not at all so fundamentally opposed to the Enlightenment as is commonly supposed. McLoughlin makes the point admirably. Baptists like Backus, he declares, "thought of their 'experimental' religion in terms which to them were just as inductive and scientific as the discoveries of Newton, Boyle, or Locke. Experimental piety . . . stated in religious terms what the Enlightenment philosophers wanted to state primarily in humanistic, secular, or rationalistic terms."[5] And what is here claimed for the American "Great Awakening" is as true of dissenting piety at just the same time in England, where for instance the great Independent Philip Dodd-ridge spoke of "experimental" religion, and seems to have meant by it just what American Baptists meant. It is not clear what happened to this concept later. But what seems certain is that Enlightenment and Dissent, which supported each other so comfortably for Isaac Back-us, had moved very far apart by 1973, when a leader of American Baptists could sum up a personal testament:

> So my conversion was a crisis of faith, the pivotal struggle in a human soul as to who prevails: Christ or culture, God or man, Jesus Christ as Sovereign Will or a people's will.[6]

The implications for a democracy, of this relegation of the "people's will," is something that I am happy to leave for U.S. citizens to worry about. My point is more simply that the choice of Christ *as against* "culture" is what, so far as I can see, Isaac Backus would not have understood and so would not have accepted; for him, if I understand him, John Locke belonged to "culture," but was not for that reason to be spurned by those who declared themselves "for Christ."

For the British on the other hand the crucial development, still little understood or remarked upon, is in the last decades of the eighteenth century the precipitate dissolution of English Presbyteri-anism into Unitarianism, either avowed or (more often) unavowed. The theological implications of this development are crucial; but in our time, when theological questions are by common consent remit-ted to experts called "theologians" (how alarmed Isaac Backus would have been!), the implications that take our eye are *political.* And here already the American and the British experiences diverge. For it is natural for Americans, citizens of a republic, to assume that a republican form of government is rational, whereas a monarchical form of government isn't. That was the view of Tom Paine, and of the many English Jacobins who would go most of the way with Paine, if not all the way. But on the other hand there were, and are, British people who hold that monarchy on the British model is just as rational, as *enlightened,* a polity as a republic is. And not only Englishmen have thought so; it was a Frenchman, Montesquieu, who taught that whereas republics depend upon the principle of civic *virtue,* monarchies inculcate and depend on the no less exalted principle of *honor.* And it seems to be Montesquieu who stands behind those lines in *The Traveller* where, emphasizing the point by a renewed address to his brother, Goldsmith deplores attempts being made to limit further under the Constitution the power of the throne, *"regal* power," the power of King George III:

> Yes, brother, curse with me that baleful hour,
> When first ambition struck at regal power;
> And thus polluting honour in its source,
> Gave wealth to sway the mind with double force.

The power of the throne, of the monarch, is here seen as a necessary bulwark for the nation at large against the otherwise unbridled power of commerce and high finance — "wealth"; against that "independence" which demands unrestricted competition in the marketplace, a free-for-all, every man for himself in the struggle for material goods and for power:

> That independence Britons prize too high,
> Keeps man from man and breaks the social tie;
> The self-dependent lordlings stand alone,
> All claims that bind and sweeten life unknown;
> Here by the bonds of nature feebly held,
> Minds combat minds, repelling and repelled.
> Ferments arise, imprisoned factions roar,
> Repressed ambition struggles round her shore,
> Till over-wrought, the general system feels
> Its motions stopped or frenzy fire the wheels.

This is the time-honored case for monarchy, which goes easily into Marxist terminology, arguing that for stability there needs to be one power in the state which stands above and outside the locked and conflicting powers of the class struggle, and that the only such power conceivable is the Crown. There are still British people, though fewer than in the past, who are monarchists on these rational grounds; and of course they do not mean by their monarchism what their American friends are eager to suppose — that the British monarchy is a charmingly ornamental and picturesque excrescence on a form of government that is, basically and essentially, as much a republican form as is the government of the United States. The changing of the guard at Buckingham Palace is a tourist attraction; but that isn't its sole nor its most important significance.

Oliver Goldsmith, to be sure, was no Dissenter, nor with any sympathies in that direction. Yet there have been religious Dissenters who held such views. How could there not have been, since English Dissenters have fought and died for their King (or Queen) and Country just as English Roman Catholics and English Anglicans have? Not all those people were stupid or befuddled about where their true interests lay. And yet the accepted account of them necessarily implies that they were, since the accepted version assumes that the Dissenters were or ought to have been, ever since Oliver Cromwell, republicans. This is for instance the implicit burden of a justly acclaimed work of American historical scholarship, Caroline Robbins's *The Eighteenth-Century Commonwealthman* (1959). That many English Dissenters of the eighteenth century did interpret in this way the heritage that they were proud to own, from the Lord Protector Cromwell and from John Milton, cannot be denied. But not all Dissenters agreed. And if they had only known (as perhaps some of them did) they could have found evidence among their colonial brethren that the Cromwellian legacy did not necessarily work in their favor. John Clarke for instance, born a Londoner in 1609, emigrated to Boston in 1637 and soon found himself rudely disenchanted by the religious intolerance of Massachusetts. Accordingly he fled for succor to the town and plantations of Providence, set up a few years earlier, as just such a refuge, by the Baptist Roger Williams. In 1651 John Clarke returned to his native London to secure from the Lord Protector Cromwell a permanent charter for all the Rhode Island communities. This task occupied John Clarke for twelve years, and when the coveted charter was at last secured it was not from Cromwell but, after Cromwell's death, from the restored monarch Charles II, in private life the most libertine of English kings but in his public policies the shrewdest and one of the most enlightened. Cromwell either evaded Clarke for eight years or else, if the petition was brought to his notice, would not accede to it; and accordingly the first of all the states to attain complete religious freedom received it from the hands of a hereditary monarch. The original charter of Rhode Island (1663) reads: "Our royal will and pleasure is, that no person within said Colony, at any time hereafter, shall be in any wise molested, punished, disquieted, or called in question for any differences of opinion in matters of religion . . . ."[7] "Our royal will and pleasure . . ." — this is Oliver Goldsmith's "regal power," actively exerted on behalf of minorities which, being outnumbered, could only have been victimized in that sort of condition called "Freedom" wherein the weakest must go to the wall. In every generation some English Dissenters have learned from this or similar instances, if not indeed from thinking politically in the abstract in the manner of John Locke, to agree with Goldsmith that the throne, the Crown, might be their surest safeguard. Before John Clarke secured the Rhode Island charter, one patriarch of English Dissent, the great Richard Baxter, had dared to say as much to Cromwell directly:

> We took our ancient monarchy to be a blessing, and not an evil to the land; and humbly craved his patience that I might ask him how England had ever forfeited that blessing, and to whom that forfeiture was made.

And in every generation of English Dissent, from Richard Baxter's to ours, there can be heard voices raised in this way, on behalf of monarchist and loyalist principles. For instance:

> The mixed form of government under which it is our distinguishing happiness to live, is the noblest monument of political wisdom and justice ever exhibited in the world. By the union of the monarchy, the aristocracy, and the democracy, we are equally protected against the tyranny of an individual, and that worst and heaviest of all scourges, the tyranny of a depraved multitude.

This is a vocabulary for politics that we are not used to: one in which "democracy" is taken to be a principle or interest in the State, neither more nor less respectable than others which are named as "aristocracy" and "monarchy." And we are not accustomed nowadays to being warned against "that worst and heaviest of all scourges, the tyranny of a depraved multitude." This is however the vocabulary of an age; as much the vocabulary of President John Adams as of Oliver Goldsmith and Edmund Burke, and of the English Dissenter whom I quote — the Congregationalist minister Edward Parsons, speaking in 1809 from his pulpit in Salem Chapel, Leeds. Now, when the agencies for depraving the multitude are so much more numerous and potent than they were in 1809 — nowadays we call them "the media" — it may well be thought that this is a vocabulary that we need to recover. However that may be, this was a vocabulary which, whatever historians may say or imply to the contrary, seemed as natural and proper to many Dissenting Christians as to Christians of the Establishment.

When the existence of this strain in English Dissent is ignored and overlooked, as it habitually is, we can be misled as William Irvine was when he told how the young South London Dissenter, Robert Browning, in the late 1820s came under the influence of the militantly atheistic and republican Shelley on the one hand, and on the other of the Unitarian minister W. J. Fox:

> . . . doctrinally, Fox was very little more (or less) than Shelley with his collar turned backward. Both held that evil was at most temporary. Both looked forward to a progress toward perfection, to an infinite felicity in some form. Shelley's atheism was not incompatible with belief in a benevolent, all-pervading Spirit. Fox believed in a God of love. Both were hostile to conventions and institutions. Both maintained that men are basically good and that to be effectually good they need first of all to be free and equal. 'There is a natural alliance,' said Fox, 'between error and slavery, truth and liberty.' In short, both men were deeply indebted to the Enlightenment.[8]

Well, so they were, both of them. No one should want to deny that Shelley's atheism and Fox's Unitarianism were products of what we call "the Enlightenment," in one of its characteristic manifestations. But on what grounds, or by what principle, do we deny the title "Enlightenment" to that course of reading which the child Browning had already pursued while still securely within the fold of his parents' Congregationalism: "Quarles' *Emblems,* Defoe's *Crusoe,* Mandeville's *Bees,* Walpole's *Letters,* 'all the works of Voltaire', Junius, many of the Elizabethans, Milton, Pope, Christopher Smart, and of course Byron"?[9]

In this list, which Irvine quotes from Browning's first and most knowledgeable biographer, Mrs. Sutherland Orr, can Quarles and Milton, the Elizabethans and Byron, outweigh the presence of such surely "Enlightenment" authors as Defoe and Mandeville, Walpole and Voltaire, Junius and Christopher Smart? And yet all of these the poet-to-be read about 1820 in the library of his solidly affluent Congregationalist parents in the London suburb of Camberwell. If "enlightened" means anything other than "infidel," how can we deny enlightenment on this showing to religious Dissenters like the Browning parents at least as late as 1820 or 1825?

Notes

1. *The Modern Language Review* 75 (January 1980), p. 165.

2. Ibid.

3. O. K. Armstrong and Marjorie Armstrong, *The Baptists in America* (New York, 1979), pp. 93, 97.

4. William G. McLoughlin, *Isaac Backus and the American Pietistic Tradition* (Boston, 1967), p. 190.

5. Ibid., p. 232.

6. *The Baptists in America*, p. 236.

7. Ibid., pp. 63 − 71.

8. William Irvine and Park Honan, *The Book, the Ring, and the Poet* (London, 1974), pp. 28 − 29.

9. Ibid., p. 7.

LECTURE THREE

Robert Browning

I have proposed — no, I have not; I have *asserted* — that whereas in the eighteenth century Dissent was a vector or a vehicle of the Enlightenment (though in ways that force us to rethink just what the "Enlightenment" was), in the nineteenth century it serves something quite other and less admirable, something indeed that much of the time is directly opposite: *un*enlightenment. In the nature of the case such a sweeping judgment cannot be demonstrated; which is the reason why I am compelled simply to assert it. The assertion can however be supported by at least circumstantial evidence. Moreover, because we are proceeding on the assumption that the most compelling evidence in all such contentions is the evidence of the arts, and because my own proclivities and training bend me towards that one of the arts which we call literature or more narrowly *poetry*, it must be in that area that we look for evidence of how in the nineteenth century Dissent became unenlightened.

And in this perspective there is no doubt what poet we must scrutinize. It is Robert Browning. Though Browning was never for long a practicing member of any Dissenting church, nevertheless Dissent was his family inheritance as it was also the inheritance of the poet he married, Elizabeth Barrett, whose poetry was in her lifetime more highly esteemed than her husband's. Browning indulged a youthful flirtation with Shelleyan atheism, but was already in retreat from that position by the time he met Elizabeth Barrett. And she, during their courtship and the first years of their famous marriage, applied herself to accelerate his retreat to the Dissent that he had imbibed at his mother's knee, that Dissent however considerably modified so as to fall in with the notably "liberal" variety that she professed herself. And here already we may and must pause: are "liberal" and "enlightened" words that go together? It is very commonly assumed that they do, but plainly the two words, like any words but these two more notably than many, are changing their meanings over the centuries; and so we may expect to find that we can with some confidence slide from one to the other when we look at certain periods of our past, but shall go very wrong if we do the same with other periods. So we ought to ask if the two words do or do not happily and justly lie down together when we try to apply them to those decades of the mid-nineteenth century when Robert and Elizabeth Barrett Browning were living and writing together. In any case there seems to be no doubt that the Brownings conceived themselves to be speaking for the tradition of English religious Dissent, though aware no doubt that they were "liberalizing" it to a point where much of Dissent would no longer want to own them. And however it may have been in their lifetimes, certainly in the decades after they had died, Dissent was proud to lay claim to them. I speak feelingly here; for it was my mother who first inculcated in me a passion for English poetry, and at her suggestion it was Browning on whom I cut my teenage teeth. It is some tribute to *her* "liberalism," both in general and more particularly as a far from overbearing or prescriptive parent, that Browning's Dissenting credentials figured not at all in her commendations of him to me, and that it was only many years later that I came to realize how her own Dissenting background had made Robert Browning stand first for her among all the English poets of all periods whom she loved.

And surely Browning is a very strong card to play, in the hand of any scion of English Dissent who wants to claim that the Dissenting tradition was alive and well in England through the reign of Queen Victoria; not just "alive" (for that we all know about, or should — the vastly increased numbers of the Dissenting faithful, and the political influence they could and did exert) but also "well" — a hale and sanative element in the public life of the nation, exerting its "clout" for the most part on behalf of decency and openness and, well, "enlightenment." Is not Browning by common consent a great poet? And does not his greatness consist very largely in the frank and masculine vigor of his imagination, the unconstrained and as it often seems unlimited range of his sympathies and his curiosity? Has he not been compared, ever since an early and splendid tribute by his friend of an older generation Walter Savage Landor, with Chaucer, no less? Yes. And it is with a sort of sorrowful deference to my mother's memory that I record my present judgment: Browning is a great poet, and at his tip-top best a Chaucerian poet, great in the way that Chaucer was great. Not the weightiest of Browning's Chaucerian performances, for instance, but among the most sparkling, is "Up at a Villa — Down in the City." However, this great Browning is the Browning furthest from Dissent, furthest from those themes and that tone which advertise him as belonging in that lineage. The more narrowly we look at Browning as a poet of religious Dissent, the worse he is. And so we can argue that, great poet though Browning is, he is none the less evidence — indeed, because of his great talents he is singularly compelling evidence — of how by the middle of the nineteenth century Dissent had become a vector of *un*enlightenment.

In passing this judgment I can call upon distinguished authority. For enlightenment was specifically denied to Browning by George Santayana, when he warned that by minds vividly responsive to what Browning has to offer, "awakening may be mistaken for enlightenment, and the galvanizing of torpid sensations and impulses for wisdom." This is in Santayana's great essay of 1900, "The Poetry of Barbarism," in which Browning on one side of the ocean and Walt Whitman on the other are declared to be not just unenlightened but positively, and quite specifically, *barbarous*:

> The "Soul" which he trusted in was the barbarous soul, the "Spontaneous Me" of his half-brother Whitman. It was a restless personal impulse, conscious of obscure depths within itself which it fancied to be infinite, and of a certain vague sympathy with wind and cloud and with the universal mutation. It was the soul that might have animated Attila and Alaric when they came down into Italy, a soul not incurious of the tawdriness and corruption of the strange civilization it beheld, but incapable of understanding its original spirit; a soul maintaining in the presence of that noble, unappreciated ruin all its own lordliness and energy, and all its native vulgarity.

Santayana's essay enjoys an odd status among us today. It is, most would agree when reminded, a classic of our criticism; and yet it is tacitly set aside whenever we approach either of the poets it deals with, or else it is treated as if it carried no more weight than any of a dozen or more academic hack jobs performed on these poets in the years since. The reason for this, I suspect, is less Santayana's harsh judgment of Browning than his even harsher dealings with Whitman; for Whitman commands more allegiance among us than Browning does, and has been emulated by many more poets, who accordingly would feel Santayana's lash curl about their shoulders as about their master's. Then, too, Santayana's tone and his vocabulary are undeniably haughty; we are democratically uneasy with a criticism that accuses a poet of "vulgarity," which speaks without embarrassment or apology of "a person coming to Browning with the habits of a cultivated mind." It isn't exactly that we deny the existence of vulgarity, or of some minds that are cultivated and others that aren't; but although we know these things, we prefer not to be reminded of them, or not at any rate in the public prints. Moreover Santayana like any one else is open to the rejoinder *ad hominem,* as when we are reminded: "So speaks a philosopher whose intellect will not allow him to accept literally and dogmatically the Catholicism for which his heart yearns, to whom it is a constant delight to remind us that Christianity rightly conceived is an ecclesiastical tradition of asceticism rather than a way of life attributed to Jesus of Nazareth."[1] And finally Santayana's way of proceeding is significantly different from that of the best modern criticism. For a good modern critic would start with observations about Browning's *style*, and move out from those to generalizations about his temperament and the cast of his mind; whereas Santayana proceeds in the opposite order. But all these concessions made, Santayana's ultimately damning judgment is surely very hard to refute:

> Apart from a certain superficial grotesqueness to which we are soon accustomed, he easily arouses and engages the reader by the pithiness of his phrase, the volume of his passion, the vigour of his moral judgment, the liveliness of his historical fancy. It is obvious

that we are in the presence of a great writer, of a great imaginative force, of a master in the expression of emotion. What is perhaps not so obvious, but no less true, is that we are in the presence of a barbaric genius, of a truncated imagination, of a thought and an art inchoate and ill-digested, of a volcanic eruption that tosses itself quite blindly and ineffectually into the sky.

And if we want corroboration, we can find it expressed in more pithy and homely phrase by one who carries even more authority than Santayana because the voice we hear is that of a great poet; one who was Browning's friend, who wrote of him as a person always with affection — Thomas Hardy:

> The longer I live, the more does B[rowning]'s character seem the literary puzzle of the 19th Century. How could smug Christian optimism worthy of a dissenting grocer find a place inside a man who was so vast a seer and feeler when on neutral ground?[2]

And Hardy there, with the word "dissenting" (which Santayana eschews), brings us back to our chief concerns, and to my reluctant contention that Browning is least the seer when he is most the Dissenter. This in turn will prompt questions about why the tradition of Dissent, which in the past had served John Bunyan and Isaac Watts so well, served Browning so ill; in short, why and how Hardy's sneer at a "dissenting grocer" is justifiable.

The principal exhibit has to be Browning's *Christmas-Eve and Easter-Day*, published April 1, 1850. Would that it were otherwise, for Browning's most fervent admirers have long been apologetic about this poem, and no one wants to bring a large-hearted poet to book for what is a wretched performance, nor to find readers for something that is in everybody's interests better left unread. But it is the poem in which Browning's sympathy with the Dissenting chapels is most explicit, and so it cannot be avoided. I shall pass over it as fast as I can, taking it as manifest that the writing, line by line, displays all of Browning's vices and few or none of his virtues. In the poem Browning takes us in imagination, on Christmas Eve of 1849, to London, to Rome, and to Göttingen. Driven by rain squalls into Zion Chapel Meeting, the speaker of the poem listens with the Dissenters to the garbling of scripture by their zealous and vociferous pastor, until the persona either falls asleep or drifts into a distracted reverie. In dream or in reverie he fancies himself transported first to St. Peter's in Rome and then to a theology lecture in Göttingen. And in this way we are invited to consider, in the context of the greatest of Christian festivals, the Dissenters' Christianity, the Roman Catholics', and finally a rationalist's. The rationalist in question was conceived very largely on the model of David Friedrich Strauss, whose *Life of Jesus Critically Examined* (1845) was to help shake or destroy the Christian faith of many eminent Victorians, including that of its translator, George Eliot. Browning's was neither shaken nor destroyed, for the sufficient reason that, as Santayana recognized, his "faith," though it comes with a great head of emotional steam behind it, has virtually no intellectual substance whatever, for Strauss or any other rationalist to unsettle. The most telling witnesses to this are precisely those who, all too faithfully following the directives of their poet, would defend *Christmas-Eve and Easter-Day*, if not as poetry exactly, at least as responsible discourse; who think that Browning can escape the strictures of Santayana or of Hoxie N. Fairchild. Thus "Browning," says Douglas Bush, "could not take historical criticism as final, because human reason and knowledge are limited and fallible and because the real evidence is within the soul." And thus, says Bush, "in spite of his antagonism to Strauss, Browning's attitude was not altogether different, though his positive faith was less intellectual and more fervent."[3] The explicit anti-intellectualism here ("less intellectual and more fervent") would obviously cut no ice with Santayana, who had specifically accused Browning of "contempt for rationality," and had declared that "a failure of reason is a failure of art and taste." The real giveaway comes with another apologist, Kingsbury Badger, who explains: "It is really not Strauss's historical demolition that Browning objects to; it is rather the purely intellectual, emotion-starved, unpoetic substitute that he offers for the Christ of the Evangelists."[4] The baleful conjunction here (and how sadly familiar it is, surely, to most of us) is of "intellectual" with "unpoetic." Poetry belongs with warm and damp "emotion," not with cold and dry "intellect" (for which read "Reason," "rationality"). Do I need to remind you how on the contrary, when we glanced in my second lecture at the Christian poetry of Christopher Smart and Charles Wesley, we had specifically to recognize "not primarily the sympathies of the human heart, but the energies of human Reason"? The difference over a century between Wesley's "Being's source begins to be,/ And God Himself is born," and Browning's "Believe in me,/ Who lived and died, yet essentially/ Am Lord of Life," is the difference between Enlightenment and unEnlightenment. In the eighteenth century our Christian poetry requires of us strenuous thinking; in the nineteenth it demands only *fervor*.

Browning's departure from orthodoxy into Shelleyan atheism, and then his wobbling back into an ambiguous and untenable no-man's-land between Belief and Unbelief, has been explained several times, chiefly by way of his emotional dependence on the two women in his life — his mother, and his wife. And undoubtedly such psychobiographical explanations have their interest and their value. But they need to be supplemented, as they seldom are, by explanations in terms of social history and the history of ideas. Such explanations would have to recreate in some detail the climate of ideas and sentiments in which lived and moved all those, like Browning's mother, who week by week sat at the feet of the Congregationalist George Clayton as he ministered to them at York Street Chapel, Walworth.[5] What seems certain is that York Street Chapel was a very different milieu from that of Zion Chapel in *Christmas-Eve and Easter-Day*; a milieu in which Robert Browning's father may not have been the only member of Mr. Clayton's congregation to have on his shelves the letters of Junius and Horace Walpole, and the works of Voltaire, Charles Avison's *Essay on Musical Expression* and Vasari's *Lives of the Painters* and Gerard de Lairesse's *The Art of Painting in All Its Branches*. It would certainly be to the point to identify George Clayton as the son of John Clayton, the Congregationalist minister who in the 1790s had earned the animosity of most of his fellow-ministers by speaking out for Pitt and for war with France, and against the English Jacobins. George Clayton, it appears, preached a Calvinism that had learned to be urbane and genteel without, however, abandoning the crucial tenets of universal depravity and salvation by faith. Early pages of Clyde Binfield's *So Down to Prayers* (London, 1977) show that there were in

England in the 1820s and 1830s many more such Calvinists than is usually supposed; Calvinists who thought themselves creatures of an Enlightenment more capacious than the one which Tom Paine and William Godwin and Mary Wollstonecraft had attempted to monopolize.

However, the Brownings by 1850 had read, or were to read, David Strauss and Bishop Colenso and Renan. If we claim Isaac Backus for the Enlightenment because he had read John Locke, or we call the eighteenth-century English Dissenters Watts and Dodd-ridge "enlightened" because they read Locke and Racine and Fénelon as well as Jonathan Edwards, how can we deny "enlighten-ment" to the Brownings who similarly studied the most advanced thinkers of their later day? It is just here that Santayana, remorse-lessly pressing home his case for the prosecution, comes to our aid: enlightenment is not a matter of what authors you read, but of the spirit you read them in:

> . . . Browning has no idea of an intelligible good which the phases of life might approach and with reference to which they might consti-tute a progress. His notion is simply that the game of life, the exhilaration of action, is inexhaustible. You may set up your tenpins again after you have bowled them over, and you may keep up the sport for ever. The point is to bring them down as often as possible with a master-stroke and a big bang. That will tend to invigorate in you that self-confidence which in this system passes for faith.

And Santayana presses the point home by attacking the Italianate Browning precisely on the score of that Italian culture which Browning declared to be the university he had studied in, after he had dropped out of that Unitarian and Dissenting institution, the infant University of London, for which his father had entered him. Browning, so Santayana claims, knew nothing of the austere and elevated level of Italian culture represented by the names of Dante and Cavalcanti, Michelangelo and Lorenzo de Medici; and here it may well be thought that Santayana goes too far — one of Brown-ing's later admirers, Ezra Pound, seems to have thought that he did.

What I need to establish is that Browning's development — from a genteel Calvinism, through Shelleyan or Unitarian optimism, to vaguely fideistic fervor — was characteristic of the best minds in

Dissent in his lifetime. And that would demand more time than I have, and more learning. I must content myself with one parallel that I hope you will find suggestive — with Thomas Binney, minister of the Weigh-house chapel in London and widely recognized in the 1850s and 1860s as the weightiest and most distinguished representative of the Dissenting churches in England. Moreover, Binney was a poet. He is at any rate the author of one poem that is not known so widely as it deserves, though it survives in our hymnbooks and is sometimes sung in protestant churches. It is a poem too about *enlightenment*, having for its epigraph one of those texts that Christians can appeal to when they refuse to let the metaphor of light be taken over by unbelievers: "The King of Kings, and Lord of lords; Who only hath immortality, dwelling in light inapproachable; Whom no man hath seen, nor can see" (1 Tim. 5: 15, 16). Binney's poem, accordingly, is entitled: "Eternal Light":

> Eternal Light! Eternal Light!
>   How pure the soul must be
> When, placed within Thy searching sight,
> It shrinks not, but with calm delight
>   Can live, and look on Thee!
>
> The Spirits that surround Thy throne
>   May bear the burning bliss;
> But that is surely theirs alone,
> Since they have never, never known
>   A fallen world like this.
>
> O how shall I, whose native sphere
>   Is dark, whose mind is dim,
> Before the Ineffable appear,
> And on my naked spirit bear
>   That uncreated beam?
>
> There is a way for man to rise
>   To that sublime abode,
> An Offering and a Sacrifice,
> A HOLY SPIRIT's energies,
>   An advocate with God:
>
> These, these prepare us for the sight
>   Of holiness above;

> The sons of ignorance and night
> May dwell in the Eternal Light,
> Through the Eternal Love.

I put this before you as an exception to the generalization I risked a few minutes ago, when I said that whereas Christian poetry in our eighteenth century required strenuous thinking, in the nineteenth it demands only fervent feeling. There is thought in Binney's admirably graceful and lucid verses; each stanza clearly enunciates a stage in a well-conducted and interesting argument; and the language, whether touchingly the language of speech as in the second stanza or more elevated and sonorous as in the third, is used responsibly. The poem is admirable in a way that modern criticism, so enamored of "complexity," pays too little heed to. And yet the burden of the poem, what it *says*, almost denies the very rationality that so clearly went into its making and its ordering. The light, we note, is *all* in heaven; there is no suggestion that the light of human Reason, fallible as it certainly is and in need of being crucially assisted by Grace, can yet take the human being *some way* towards those crystalline apprehensions which (we admit) are constantly available only to the blest in Eternity. Our native sphere is said to be "dark," and our minds "dim." And so they are, of course; yet we do have the light of Reason to illuminate us, however fitfully. And this is something that Binney's poem leaves out of account. In doing so, it repudiates the belief and aspiration of the Enlightenment.

And in this way we begin to see how the author of this poem could also have expressed himself, less attractively, as follows:

> A whole world-full of modern men, with the thoughts to think and the work to do belonging to their age, have been obliged to listen for weeks and months to the jargon of the schools, to metaphysical distinctions and theological niceties that *they* can only regard as important who draw the pabulum of their internal life from the past — *man*'s past, not God's — the times of councils and popes and priests, who suspended eternity on whatever attached importance to themselves! Why, who cares what this council, or that, or the other, thought or determined? What is it to us, who have got something else to think about and do, in this nineteenth century of

the Christian redemption (and society nothing like redeemed yet), than to hear what was thought, hundreds of years ago, on matters, it may be, which nobody believes, or about which we can judge better ourselves than any old ecclesiastical conclave could judge for us?[6]

This is the voice not of any run-of-the-mill Dissenting rabble-rouser but of the author of "Eternal Light"; the man who boldly rethought and reformulated a social role for Congregationalism in his day, and also a liturgy for it; the man who under a pseudonym was singled out for commendation in *The Revolution in Tanner's Lane* (1887), that Victorian novel which is most inward with English Nonconformity, written by the very wary and critical and admirable man who wrote under the pseudonym, "Mark Rutherford." Before Binney died there had appeared the most searing indictment, by a Victorian, of the characteristic temper of Victorian Nonconformity. This was Matthew Arnold's *Culture and Anarchy* (1869), in which the Victorian Dissenters are assailed as the principal carriers of the virus that Arnold calls "philistinism," thereby creating the meaning that "philistine" and "philistinism" have for us today. And the voice that says, "We can judge better ourselves than any old ecclesiastical conclave could judge for us," is the very voice of Matthew Arnold's *philistine*. It comes as no surprise that Binney's admiring Victorian biographer should jauntily concede that he had probably never read Jonathan Edwards; or that the sectarian journal of the time, *The Nonconformist*, should in its obituary of Binney give him credit for having cleared out "much of the ancient dispensation, handed down through six generations of Dissenters." Binney's voice is hard to distinguish, surely, from that of the American Baptist leader whom we heard, in 1973, opting for Christ *as against* "culture."

What Arnold stigmatized as "philistine" in *Culture and Anarchy* (elsewhere his word for it is "provincial") is a quality of *tone;* and accordingly it's something which, if people cannot hear it for themselves, they cannot be convinced of. It is to be heard, surely, in what has just been quoted from Thomas Binney — a tone that is brutal, overemphatic, overconfident: "Why, who cares . . . this council, or that, or the other . . . What is it to us . . . something else to think about and do . . . we can judge better . . ." Many Victorians seem to have heard it, this tone of voice, as manly, as hearty — in the sense of heartfelt and wholehearted; it seemed to them to have the authority of Thomas Carlyle, and indeed it is surely with Carlyle that it originates. It is certainly not peculiar to Nonconformists, but is to be heard for instance in Dickens (who by the way traduced Binney unforgivably), and oddly enough even in Arnold himself at times. It is the voice at all periods, including our own, of "modern men, with the thoughts to think and the work to do belonging to their age." It is, above all, impatient and therefore irreverent. And it is certainly to be heard at times in Browning, as in Charles Kingsley, where Gerard Manley Hopkins heard it and characterized it unforgivingly but vividly when he envisaged a man starting up from the breakfast table, his mouth full of bacon and eggs, declaring that he will stand no damn'd nonsense.

Some who can hear this tone, and are even (a little) offended by it, believe that they can excuse it away by fastening on Arnold's alternative word, "provincial." Even leaving aside the literally geographical sense of "provincial," which can provoke from English people angry or scornful rejoinders about snobbish gentilities of the Home Counties and Oxbridge, apologists for Nonconformity can take the figurative meaning that Arnold attached to the word, the meaning of "far from the center" — far from that center, not locatable on any map, where standards (of social and intellectual behavior) are set up and kept up. What is that center (so English Dissenters may ask) if not the Establishment, in England the Church of England? And in this way it is possible to protest that Matthew Arnold berates Nonconformists (Dissenters) for not having access to just that center which he, as a guardian of the Establishment, has carefully debarred them from. It is a defense, no doubt; but hardly one that English Dissenters can take much pride in. And it is in any case untrue to history. For as Dr. Johnson recognized when he wrote about the great Dissenter Isaac Watts (in his *Lives of the Poets*), Dissent in Watts's lifetime, and largely thanks to Watts himself, had contrived to get access to that civilized center, that imaginary academy, despite its sectarian status. Through Isaac Watts and a few other Dissenting leaders like him, Dissenting Christianity had contrived to participate in that great movement in the mind of Western man which we call, when we think about it, "the Enlightenment"; and that Dissenting yet Enlightenment culture survived in England into the first years of the reign of Queen Victoria. But what later Dissenters thought of it appears from how Paxton Hood, Binney's Victorian biographer, characterized the regime at the King's Weigh-house of John Clayton, Binney's predecessor there: "a kind of florid frost-work, in which religious truth was held in a cold crystallization of sanctified Chesterfieldism, for ever fearing to offend." The obituary in *The Nonconformist* had struck the same note in less Carlylean idiom, saying that Binney came to the King's Weigh-house when "the age of silk and lavender, and of successful suppression of thought under decorous phrases, was coming to an end." Nineteenth-century Dissenters *did not want,* they contemptuously threw away, the civility and the enlightenment that eighteenth-century Dissent had achieved. And Robert Browning, though he surely never confronted the issue in just these terms nor made any conscious decision about it, is nevertheless infected by this climate of opinion, and disabled by it more than a little.

Santayana says that "the essential conception of any rational philosophy" is "that feeling is to be treated as raw material for thought, and that the destiny of emotion is to pass into objects which shall contain all its value while losing all its formlessness." And he declares: "This transformation of sense and emotion into objects agreeable to the intellect, into clear ideas and beautiful things, is the natural work of reason; . . ." This is a view of "reason" for which we can find no room so long as we are hung up on a dichotomy between intellect supposedly "cold" and feeling or emotion supposedly "warm." To the Victorians it seemed that the rationalism of the Enlightenment had produced systems of thought that were indeed "cold": atheism, Unitarianism, utilitarianism. And a Victorian like Browning, appalled by the chill that came up from these systems, opted instead for the warmth of feelings that Browning was content *not* to have transformed into "clear ideas and beautiful things." Many of us, more than a century later, are on the horns of this same false dilemma, and opt for Browning's solution or evasion. Santayana speaks to us, if we are prepared to listen, by showing that the dilemma is indeed a false one, since "rationality" is something altogether more ample than "rationalism."

It is because we, in our art and our morals and politics, need rather desperately to learn this lesson, that we cannot shuffle off or set aside Santayana's condemnation of Browning in the light of these principles. All the same, those of us who are most persuaded by Santayana's argument as a whole may properly rebel at some of his particular judgments. This one, for instance:

> Love is depicted by Browning with truth, with vehemence, and with the constant conviction that it is the supreme thing in life. The great variety of occasions in which it appears in his pages and the different degrees of elaboration it receives, leave it always of the same quality — the quality of passion. It never sinks into sensuality; in spite of its frequent extreme crudeness, it is always, in Browning's hands, a passion of the imagination, it is always love. On the other hand it never rises into contemplation: mingled as it may be with friendship, with religion, or with various forms of natural tenderness, it always remains a passion; it always remains a personal impulse, a hypnotization, with another person for its object or its cause.

We may agree that this is a true description of how Browning treats of love between the sexes and still feel that Browning's achievement in this area deserves far more credit than Santayana will accord it. To stay faithful to passion, without falling on the one hand into sensuality or taking wing on the other hand into some sort of sublimation — we, who have seen how hard it is to maintain this balance, may well feel admiring gratitude to Browning, especially when we recall how many of his most glowing and ardent love-poems (I will instance just one, the beautifully tender "One Word More") are poems of married love. Some of us are more aware than Santayana seems to have been, of how often apparent sublimations of sexual passion mask impulses of domination and appropriation of the beloved by the lover. Moreover it's by no means clear that Browning was unaware of those Santayana calls "the real masters of passion and imagination," for whom "the sudden self-surrender in which he rests was . . . the starting-point of a life of rational worship," for whom therefore "love ceased to be a passion and became the energy of contemplation." With two such "masters," Dante and Michelangelo, Browning seems to have had dealings far more intimate than Santayana allows for. A later poet who was proud to subscribe himself one of Browning's poetic sons ("Pourquoi nier son père?" he said) seems to have been prepared to defend Browning on this flank. This was Ezra Pound, who speaks with authority since he probed behind Dante and Cavalcanti in search of this love that is "the energy of contemplation," and located it in the "AMOR" of those Provençal poets whom Dante confessedly learned from; and accordingly no poem by Browning matters more to Pound than the long and early "Sordello," in which Browning treats of a Provençal poet of Mantua.

However that may be, no one need feel ashamed of discovering in Browning a model of love between the sexes, especially love within wedlock, more worthy of emulation than any model that has been provided since. And of course this model or image is particularly potent because it is mirrored not just in Browning's writings but in his life also, so that it influences people who are not students of literature. The famous "romance" of his courtship of Elizabeth Barrett, and of how like Perseus he released that Andromeda from her rock and from her dragon of a father, has of course been simplified and falsified into soap opera. But the primary documents — Elizabeth Barrett's love letters and her "Sonnets from the Portuguese," as well as her husband's letters and poems — are still available and resonant for those who want to go to the sources. We shall next be concerned with a living British poet for whom these documents resound very loudly indeed.

Notes

1. Kingsbury Badger, "'See the Christ stand!': Browning's Religion," *Boston University Studies in English*, 1 (1955 – 6). In P. Drew (ed.), *Robert Browning: A Collection of Critical Essays* (Boston, 1966) p. 75.

2. Quoted by Kingsbury Badger, ibid., p. 73.

3. Bush, *Science and English Poetry* (London: Oxford, 1950), p. 132. Quoted by Badger, ibid., p. 87.

4. Ibid.

5. See his *Course of Sermons on Faith and Practice Delivered at York Street Chapel, Walworth, 1838 – 39* (London, 1839).

6. E. Paxton Hood, *Thomas Binney: His Mind, Life, and Opinions* (London, 1874), p. 33. (All subsequent quotations are from this source).

Two of Browning's Heirs

The British poet Jack Clemo begins his autobiography published
this year (*The Marriage of a Rebel* [London, 1980]) as follows:

> On a Saturday afternoon in July 1947 a small grey-haired woman
> stood at the tomb of Robert Browning in Westminster Abbey.
> Through horn-rimmed spectacles her large black eyes probed the
> shadowy carvings and slabs of Poets' Corner with the nervousness
> of a country-dweller who was paying her first visit to London. She
> was alone, and there was an atmosphere of solitude about her: one
> could not imagine her as a woman who had many friends. It was as
> though she had spent most of her life grappling with situations so
> unusual that in her attempts to understand and deal with them she
> had lost touch with her prosaic working-class neighbours, and with
> the trends and interests of her own generation. Her sallow face,
> which had never been softened by cosmetics, was deeply lined with
> suffering, and the big nose and determined jaw suggested that
> strength of character had developed in her at the expense of su-
> perficial charm. But there was no bitterness in her expression. As
> she bent forward to read the inscription on Browning's tomb her
> face relaxed in a sort of bewildered gratitude.
>   The woman was my mother, Eveline Clemo. . . .

And Jack Clemo goes on to explain that the suffering which had
grooved his mother's face was largely involved with her caring for
her physically afflicted son, himself, whereas her bewildered gratitude to Browning (whom she had hardly read) was because it was
from Browning that her son had derived the sustaining conviction
that despite his afflictions he would become an author, and that his
writing would be bound up, as Browning's was, with happy marriage. Then, in 1947, the first of these unlikely aspirations had been
realized, with the acceptance of Clemo's novel, *Wilding Graft,* of

which both the title and the motto were taken from Browning's poems; but the second consummation, marriage, was still twenty years in the future.

Jack Clemo is a poet hardly known in the U.S. though it is twenty years since Daniel Hoffman published a poem about him in the *Transatlantic Review*. His afflictions have been dwelt upon more than he likes; for understandably he resents being presented as a sort of prodigious freak. Briefly, he has been throughout his life intermittently and partially (of late almost totally) blind and deaf. What is more to the point is that he is as authentic a *proletarian* author as modern Britain has produced; and that he is also in our time perhaps the most authentic and distinguished poet to come out of, and to speak for, English Dissenting Protestantism.

The Marriage of a Rebel, which is subtitled portentously but accurately "A Mystical-erotic Quest," is not Clemo's first essay in autobiography. It had been preceded by *Confession of a Rebel* (1949) and by *The Invading Gospel* (1958). No one of these books can be ignored. All can be considered, if we care to take them that way, as necessary commentaries on Clemo's poetry. And it may be objected that poetry of the best sort does not need, does not so depend on, extraneous elucidation by the poet. The objection is just, but it should not be pressed very far. For this poet emerges from, and articulates, a cultural situation so special, both personally and historically, that it is not the poet's fault but rather the fault of avoidable ignorance on our part, if a context for his poems has to be laboriously supplied — and by the poet himself, if no one else volunteers. It has been the assumption, and in part the burden, of these lectures, that the cultural tradition which this poet speaks from — Dissenting Christianity — is habitually and improperly considered, in Britain as in the U.S., as an "underground" tradition, about which the most total ignorance is excusable. But in any case Clemo's Dissenting inheritance, and also his physical disabilities, are only the start; he cuts athwart our expectations in all sorts of other ways. For instance, the sheer fact of his Englishness is in some degree open to question. He is, and not by accident but by inheritance, a Cornishman, a son of that southwestern peninsula of England where he has always lived and lives still, where the inhabitants are well aware of themselves as a Celtic people having ethnically less in common with the English than with the Welshmen of Wales and the Bretons of Britanny, that northwestern peninsula of France which the Cornish in the Dark Ages imperially colonized. Thus Clemo's is a special case in all sorts of ways; and yet I believe he supports and illustrates the thesis that I am urging.

In the first place there can be no doubt that he is an heir of Robert Browning. *The Marriage of a Rebel* tells us how the dog whose companionship meant much to Clemo through some of his most desolate years was named by him "Plush" after the famous lapdog of Elizabeth Barrett; and the same narrative shows Clemo giving superstitious attention to how the dates of momentous events in his own life corresponded, on the calendar, with dates in the records of the Brownings' courtship and marriage. The internal evidence of his poems tells the same story: a poem called "The Brownings at Vallombrosa" fittingly illustrates, among a score of other instances, how some idiosyncrasies of Browning's writing — notably, in meter, a headlong readiness to substitute trisyllabic for disyllabic feet, and an obtrusive rhyming which, while it doesn't determine or divert meaning, still draws attention to itself too flagrantly to satisfy such as Santayana — are features of Clemo's practice also. Like Browning Clemo not only is, but seeks to be, in his writing craggy, roughhewn, volcanic. Accordingly we need not expect to find him recovering for the Dissenting tradition that sinewy yet suave polish which it had known, in the Enlightenment, at the hands of Isaac Watts:

> Hosanna to the royal son
> Of David's ancient line!
> His natures two, his person one,
> Mysterious and divine . . .

No, this is not Clemo's tone at all. And in fact he is very categorical and explicit about this, as we might expect from a writer so self-conscious. In *Confession of a Rebel* he declares:

> It was impossible for me ever to take the cultured, civilized view of human rights — or of anything else. I demanded Christian gusto and scorned the weary dignity of the classic ideal. Ever since my childhood I had detested the Greek spirit and loved the Gothic. . . .

And in *The Invading Gospel* he confesses that "I liked Wesley's hymns and much of his *Journal,* but his sermons seemed to me as chilled by eighteenth-century rationality as the writings of Edwards and Haldane." This antipathy to *rationality* (not just to "rationalism"), which Clemo finds as offensive in the Calvinist Jonathan Edwards as in the Arminian John Wesley, warns us clearly not to look in him for a remarriage between the Dissenting heritage and "the Enlightenment." On the other hand, though his demand for what he calls "Christian gusto" is constant with him, and fervent — he was perhaps the only British man of letters, certainly the only British poet, to respond with enthusiasm to the evangelist Billy Graham — it would not be true to say of him what we have to say much of the time, regretfully, of Browning: that his Christian faith is all fervent feeling, with no intellectual substance. On the contrary there is surely nobility as well as pathos in the story he tells of how, a penurious autodidact in enforced isolation, he became aware in the late 1940s of the achievement of the great Swiss theologian Karl Barth, who regenerated for our time the Calvinist doctrines which the young Clemo had imbibed, mutinously sometimes, at the knee of his mother, bred in the Calvinist variant of Methodism which has always been particularly strong in Cornwall. *The Invading Gospel* is the one of his autobiographies which brings out most clearly how Clemo's Dissent had intellectual sinews, such as Browning's hadn't. And the processional stateliness of Clemo's poem, "On the Death of Karl Barth," movingly commemorates the great theologian and trailbreaker.

If we say of this, as we might of other poems by Clemo, that it and they are quite unlike other modern poems in English, we may seem to be claiming for their author only the status of an oddity, a curio, perhaps an anomalous survivor. And it is true that none of the categories that usually serve us well with modern poets — "symbolist" or "post-symbolist," "imagist" or "post-imagist," "objectivist" or "objectist," indeed not even the capacious category "modernist" itself — will help us with this body of poetry. Neither "symbol" nor "image" will help us because the habit of Clemo's imagination is constantly and indelibly *allegorical.* Those of us who remember *Maule's Curse,* the late Yvor Winters's study of the Calvinist sensibility in New England, will remember how Winters argued that the allegorical habit — the reading of experience for clues and signs to the Divine purpose — was in that culture endemic and inescapable. Clemo's reading of his own experience is always of this kind; and though his poems are crowded with sensuous details in a way remarkable for a poet whose senses were impaired, those details are to be read in a way quite different from anything we are used to in the symbolist or the imagist ways of writing: every sensuous detail has to be (and usually is, explicitly) *decoded,* allegorically. And before we jump to the conclusion that this is a way of experiencing that we all left behind in seventeenth-century Massachusetts, we need to pause and think whether, for good or ill, this way of reading the universe for "signs" is not inculcated at the present time, week by week, in various protestant communions, Baptist and other, where, so we may conjecture, this allegorizing habit is still the staple intellectual activity, alike in the pulpit and out of it.

Clemo's finest poem, I think, is his "Mould of Castile," dedicated to St. Teresa of Avila, and closely related throughout to what we know of Teresa's life (1515 – 82). And incidentally this is only the best of several poems in which Clemo, nonconformist protestant though he is, pays tribute to saints of the Roman Church; "oecumenical" is what he has always been, in the sense of being ready to go to any Christian Church at all to get the spiritual nourishment that he needs. (It's in this spirit that he can pay tribute to the Anglican C. S. Lewis: "He was no Calvinist, but Calvinism is a statement of how Christianity works, and fellowship rests on an agreement as to what Christianity is.") In "Mould of Castile" Clemo has unshackled himself from all Browningesque precedents in the use of rhyme, meter, and stanza structure:

> A streak of Sappho, it is said,
> Inflamed you, the painted and imperious
> Charmer in velvet robes at Avila;
> But soon your withered young bones rattled
> On convent stones: gaunt postulant,
> You had fled, still dead to God, from a goblin-flare.

No mist or dream had softened
The bold Castilian flint: there was sun-glare
On bull-fights and flashing lizards
And the hot black stems of olives, pungent cistus,
Awaiting the shift and shock, an El Greco storm.

Did you waste thirty years
In fighting the sun, flashing out
With a gay jest between swoons and fears
Of those winged visions? Did election dare
Molest your Spanish pride
To that length, fan a fury of love
That soared, bled in the trap,
Lapped a wilful ease, lastly, in brisk reform?

You were ageing, an enigma still,
When your mules arrived at San Jose,
And a thunder that thrills my flint
In Cornwall now, spread from the wooden waggons,
Filled with your nuns, lurching over calcined plains,
Up primitive mountain-tracks, drifting aground
On river ferries. You and they were bound
For new cells in Elisha's shadow:
Traditional rock like that which my poet-soul,
As wasted and adamant,
Split and gay as yours, descried
Beyond sly bramble, misted kiln
And the dried voluptuary veins.

It should be clear that in this poem the landscape of Castile
(which of course the poet had never seen), with its characteristic
light and color, is to be interpreted neither symbolically nor imagis-
tically but allegorically or else emblematically — as is, in the last
two lines, the terrain of that industrially mutilated landscape, the
China-clay district of Cornwall where Clemo was born and has
lived, unresentfully, ever since.

"Mould of Castile" and also "On the Death of Karl Barth"
appeared — along with other instructive pieces like "Porthmeor
Cemetery" and "Mary Shelley in Geneva" and "Cookworthy at
Carloggas" — in Clemo's collection of 1971, *The Echoing Tip*. His
next collection, which is his last to date, *Broad Autumn* (1975),

contains other pieces that are striking and memorable. Among these is "Royal Wedding," about the wedding of the Princess Anne, an occasion that Clemo was party to by way of radio or else television, and thanks to the assistance of his own late-found and devoted wife. This poem, though it includes patches of weak writing, is interesting because it shows how a proletarian religious Dissenter like Clemo can be a sincerely patriotic monarchist, can find significance and alleviation for his own condition by participating in the rituals of the monarchy. This contention — as I prefer to say, this truth — is very unwelcome to many people in England. On the one hand are those who are or conceive themselves to be of the governing class, to whom it rather commonly seems that properly monarchical sentiments are available only to members of that church, the Church of England, of which the monarch is the head. And on the other hand are those more or less *marxisant* politicians and educators and historians who take it for granted that an unprivileged proletarian like Clemo must nurse sentiments that are antimonarchist, if not republican, at all events socialist.

You will have noticed that Clemo explicitly and with a heavy hand relates the situation of St. Teresa to his own situation. And with him this is normal. Places and people, however remote from Jack Clemo, are in his poems sooner or later connected directly and quite explicitly with himself in his own landscape of Cornwall. This is inevitable, given the allegorical cast of his imagination; people and places are scrutinized for clues and keys — and to what if not to himself, his own spiritual and cultural condition? This means that his poetry is very self-centered. How could it be otherwise? Since physical circumstance and historical accident have placed Clemo in a universe so special that hardly anyone shares it with him, how could he not put himself at the center of it? The consequence is, however, that he is very far from sharing a characteristic emphasis of the modernist poetry we associate with the name of T. S. Eliot — that is to say, the aspiration towards a poetry that shall be *im*personal, a product of the English language and of the English-speaking peoples, rather than of any one speaker of that language at any one time. To be sure, in this Clemo is not unlike other authors who are sometimes called "modernist" — D. H. Lawrence, for example, who at one time meant much to him. But this has had the effect of closing to Clemo one kind of poem to which his nonconformist background might have seemed to give him privileged access — the poem that is a hymn. For the congregational hymn, precisely because it is composed so as to be uttered not by an individual but by a congregation or by many congregations, is therefore necessarily, and in a very obvious sense, *impersonal.* This was recognized by Eliot himself, who linked the hymn with (surprisingly) the epigram, saying of both that they are "extremely objective types of verse." Accordingly, neither hymn nor epigram is to be found in the poetry of Jack Clemo. Both are to be found however in the work of another of Browning's heirs: Rudyard Kipling. It was with Kipling in mind that T. S. Eliot was led to this reflection. And Rudyard Kipling is the next of the modern poets whom I want to consider — another poet who, though undoubtedly "modern," is certainly not "modernist," another poet with whom categories like "symbolist" and "imagist" get us nowhere at all.

Kipling of course is a famous riddle; and accordingly he has attracted the attention not just of Eliot but of others among the most powerful and fearless minds of our time, Edmund Wilson and Lionel Trilling, George Orwell and Randall Jarrell and Angus Wilson. I will be bold enough to suggest that the riddle is less riddling than some of these distinguished minds have made out. For instance, Edmund Wilson's momentous essay of 1941, "The Kipling that Nobody Read," rests on the assumption that Kipling's account of his own boyhood is so tightlipped as to be dishonest; and if we find on the contrary that in Kipling's fragmentary and incomplete autobiography, *Something of Myself* (1937), the account of his boyhood in all its reticence rings true, then most of Wilson's argument slips down like a house of cards. More generally, as I am not the first to notice, the riddle of Kipling is largely created by liberal and humanitarian critics who have decided, without noticing, that literary genius can be allowed to happen only among people who share their social and political sentiments. They suppose that imperialists and racists are, by definition, stupid; Kipling, who was imperialist and racist, wasn't stupid at all, nor philistine either — hence the riddle, which is a riddle only to those political "liberals" whom Kipling consistently baited and deliberately affronted throughout his writing life. This, we may begin to suspect, is one of those cases where "liberal" points one way, and "enlightened" points another.

Kipling was not a son or heir of Robert Browning in quite the straightforward way that we have seen with Jack Clemo. Kipling, no one denies, was astonishingly precocious; and also he profited by exceptionally enlightened schooling (though his grateful acknowledgment of that is another testimony that his critics refuse to accept). Accordingly, almost from the first Browning's influence had to be combined with, or find its place among, the numerous other literary precedents that the omnivorous schoolboy was astonishingly aware of. Nevertheless the primacy of Browning (taking precedence even over Swinburne, whom Eliot makes much of) is sufficiently attested by for instance C. E. Carrington's standard biography, and it shows up, as Carrington astutely notes, not only in poems but in the structure of some of the early and famous stories. Now, Browning was capable of writing poems that are, by whatever standard, objective and impersonal; as witness for instance his much loved yet underrated "Cavalier Tunes," which were to serve Ezra Pound memorably when Pound was translating some poems of ancient China. Yet in Browning, despite his nonconformist background, such impersonal lyrics never took the form of hymns or of poems that are hymnlike. Accordingly we look in vain in Browning for anything that points to Kipling's hymn or hymnlike "Recessional" of 1897, perhaps the most famous of all his poems:

> God of our fathers, known of old,
>   Lord of our far-flung battle-line,
> Beneath whose awful Hand we hold
>   Dominion over palm and pine —
> Lord God of Hosts, be with us yet,
> Lest we forget — lest we forget!

Here we encounter, as distinct from the largely factitious "riddle" of Kipling, one of the many authentic mysteries about him: when, where, and from whom did he imbibe that awesomely wide yet exact familiarity with the idiom of the Old Testament (in the King

James version, of course) which lends authority and resonance to a poem like this, just as it does to its unregarded and orthodox ancestors, hymns by Isaac Watts and Charles Wesley? (The same authority, and the same resonance, are earned by poems that are not hymnlike at all, as well as by many of the famous stories.) To this question, so far as I can see, neither Kipling's own memoirs nor the reputable biographies provide any answer. After all, it is not as if Kipling grew up in a God-fearing and church-going family; on the contrary, Kipling's parents had lapsed from an ancestral Methodism to the point where they very seldom attended any church at all, and equally seldom we may suppose read Scripture together. Where then did the knowledge of Scripture come from? May we dare to suppose that it came from her who is the villain of the story according to Edmund Wilson (though not according to Kipling) — the ogress of Southsea, the cruel foster-mother (described as "Evangelical" and "Calvinist," as if the terms were interchangeable) with whom the young Rudyard was boarded out while his parents remained in India? Perish the thought! And yet the question remains: where did Rudyard Kipling, embarrassingly anti-Semite at times in his later life, imbibe his conception of certain races as "chosen of God," as the "elect," if not from the Hebrew scriptures of the Old Testament?

I ought to make it clear where I stand, as regards this so celebrated "Recessional." It is a poem right enough, a masterly one. It belongs with poetry, not (where Eliot would put it) in a vaguely undefined but somehow subordinate category called "verse," still less in that fatuous *ad hoc* category dreamed up by George Orwell, "good bad poetry." "Recessional" is a poem, a very *wicked* poem. And I call it wicked not because it enunciates relations between the races of mankind such as I myself do not hold by (and yes, to be sure, we know that "the lesser breeds without the law" are white Germans, not brown Afghans); but for more strictly artistic reasons — because a form of poetry consecrated to the celebration of Christian charity (as that Charity could and was understood by Isaac Watts and his first auditors) is here perverted to the purposes of *un*Charity. Another way of saying this is that Kipling in this poem coldbloodedly and expertly touched one after another of the stops that would move an audience of Christian Believers into sympathy with himself, who was a cynical Unbeliever. Nothing is more astonishing — and yet nothing, given the present benign muddle about the boundary between Belief and Unbelief, is more logical — than that this poem, this most shocking of all Kipling's utterances, should be habitually exempted from criticism by those commentators who on other grounds bear hardest on him.

Did Kipling in any case belong to, or have any feelingful connection with, that tradition in English culture which we have identified as "Dissent"? Edmund Wilson and some other commentators have made much of the fact that his grandfathers on both sides were Methodist ministers; and his cousin Stanley Baldwin, later Prime Minister of Great Britain, declared on one occasion that this inheritance that he shared with Kipling made both of them heirs to a "puritan" tradition. But once again we may as well trust Kipling himself, who in *Something of Myself* spoke of this Wesleyan tradition in his family as something presented to him only late, and as it were in passing. In any case, it is not at all clear that the Wesleyan (Methodist) persuasion in English history belongs with the Dissenting, the Nonconformist, strain. There are those who will maintain vociferously that it does not, so late come as it is, and, during the lives of the Wesley brothers, so determined not to secede from the Church of England in which it began. The truth seems to be that a Methodist in England is a Dissenter, a Nonconformist, only if he chooses so to regard himself, or so to acquiesce in the opinion that his Anglican neighbors have of him. Jack Clemo declares outright (*The Marriage of a Rebel*, p. 65) that he conceived his Calvinistic Methodism as making of him a Nonconformist. But there is no evidence that the inherited Methodism of the Kiplings and the Baldwins led them to think of themselves in any such light. It was useful to them, however, as a sort of fall-back position, when they got themselves into quandaries and self-contradictions which only a profession of Nonconformity or of "puritanism" could get them out of. This seems to have happened to Kipling at the time of the war in South Africa, when his poems about that war make such rhetorical play with heroes of the Nonconformist tradition, such as Bunyan and Cromwell. The exceptionally implausible special pleadings that this let him in for is something I have examined elsewhere;[1] and it is all part of the background of "Recessional." Even in *Something of Myself*, and certainly in the poems and stories, there is evidence that the Boer War, the war in South Africa, was what coarsened and rigidified Kipling's ideas and made him more or less consciously prostitute his art. From this rigidity, and from this prostitution, the First World War, in which he lost his only son, shocked him back though less than perfectly.

Though Edmund Wilson is wrongheaded, and also surprisingly ignorant about the *mores* of the British propertied classes before 1914, nevertheless his essay, "The Kipling That Nobody Read," has the merits of living up to its title and of directing attention to the neglected older Kipling, post-1918. Wilson however was concerned for the storyteller of those years, not the poet. And a case is to be made for the aging Kipling as a poet. This is the Kipling who is drawn not to the hymn but to the other of the "objective" and "impersonal" forms that Eliot identified — the epigram. And Eliot duly included in his *Choice of Kipling's Verse* (1941) the very fine and harrowing sequence, "Epitaphs of the War." But the virtues of the epigram inform some other poems, Landorian or Horatian or both, that are too long to be called epigrams proper; and these Eliot represented less generously. In particular he seems to have disapproved of the harmless hoax that Kipling cooked up with the help of A. D. Godley, Orator of Oxford University, when he issued what purported to be translations from a nonexistent Book V of Horace's Odes. And yet some of these poems are a great deal better and more serious than mere japes. It is very interesting to learn from C. E. Carrington that Horace's Odes, more specifically Book III of them, which he was made to study by his schoolmaster F. W. Haslam, is pretty well the only text from ancient Greek or Latin which Kipling knew in the original. (Unlike Browning before him, or the self-educated Thomas Hardy, Kipling knew no classical Greek at all, and little Latin; this is one seldom noticed way in which Kipling was very "modern" indeed — at his school, which was, as he rightly said, "before its time," English literature was made to serve the purpose that, through the centuries since the Renaissance, Greek and Latin literature had served. Kipling knows

English literature so well because he knows classical literature so little, and in the generations before him there are very few English poets of whom this is true.) At any rate Horace, and the Horatian tone in verse, came to mean much to him. It can be detected as early as 1901, in "The Reformers"; but most of the poems in this chiselled lapidary manner belong to the years after 1918. One, dated 1920, is "Lollius," which belongs with the "spoof" translations, and accordingly does not appear in Eliot's *Choice*:

> Why gird at Lollius if he care
>   To purchase in the city's sight,
> With nard and roses for his hair,
>   The name of Knight?
>
> Son of unmitigated sires
>   Enriched by trade in Afric corn,
> His wealth allows, his wife requires,
>   Him to be born.
>
> Him slaves shall serve with zeal renewed
>   At lesser wage for longer whiles,
> And school- and station-masters rude
>   Receive with smiles.
>
> His bowels shall be sought in charge
>   By learned doctors; all his sons
> And nubile daughters shall enlarge
>   Their horizons.
>
> For fierce she-Britons, apt to smite
>   Their upward-climbing sisters down,
> Shall smooth their plumes and oft invite
>   The brood to town.
>
> For these delights will he disgorge
>   The State enormous benefice,
> But — by the head of either George —
>   He pays not twice!
>
> Whom neither lust for public pelf,
>   Nor itch to make orations, vex —
> Content to honour his own self
>   With his own cheques —
>
> That man is clean. At least, his house
>   Springs cleanly from untainted gold —

> Not from a conscience or a spouse
>   Sold and resold.
>
> Time was, you say, before men knew
>   Such arts, and rose by Virtue guided?
> The tables rock with laughter — you
>   Not least derided.

This represents a sort of poetry so different from what we have become used to that some of us not only take no pleasure in it, but actually cannot make sense of it. It may for all we know be aimed at a particular person, though I think not. On the other hand, of the two "Georges" in stanza 6, if one is King George V, who was or became Kipling's friend, the other is surely David Lloyd George, Kipling's political enemy, who notoriously when in power "sold" peerages and other civil distinctions. "Lollius," who has thus bought his title with money acquired as a war profiteer, is declared in the poem to be more of a fair dealer than others in the State — the orating politicians who sold it to him, or even it may be those with more ancient titles who have preserved their aristocratic status by "a conscience or a spouse/ Sold and resold." What is more important is to recognize how the tersely neat Horatian procedures convey a disgusted detachment more lethal than the vehement indignation which had spurred a younger Kipling to fulminate against "the flannelled fools at the wicket or the muddied oafs at the goals"; and how the same procedures wearily concede that the scoundrelism the poem talks of is not peculiar to Britain in 1920 but is the squalid same through the centuries, how therefore no progress is made. Of many incidental felicities, I would draw attention to two. The first is the very elegant Latinism in line 5, "unmitigated" (from the Latin *mitis*, "mild"), where the meaning of "mitigate" is the one which OED notes as "now rare" — "To render (a person, *etc.*) milder; to appease, mollify." Thus the one word, "unmitigated," conveys that Lollius is the first of his family to be ennobled, and at the same time exposes contemptuously what it is that people get ennobled *for*, i.e. to be bought over, to have their fangs drawn. And the second fine stroke to be noted is the extraordinarily deft allusion, at the turn from the seventh into the eighth stanza, to Alexander Pope's Horatian "Ode on Solitude":

> Happy the man, whose wish and care
> A few paternal acres bound,
> Content to breathe his native air
> In his own ground.

Substituting "With his own cheques" for "In his own ground" brilliantly encapsulates 200 years of history which saw England change from being a predominantly landed and agrarian culture into one that is predominantly financial and commercial. It was a historical process that Pope himself saw the start of, in the England of Robert Walpole. To get so much said, simply by making one cadence echo another over two centuries, seems not much short of miraculous.

Such effects, achieved with such disdainful and self-effacing economy, are not to be met with in any of the several styles that Robert Browning practiced, and of course they are wholly inconceivable in any of the innumerable Browningesque or Whitmanesque poetasters of our own day. So do we not have at last, in this joining of hands with Pope, a case of Dissenting Christianity joining up again with the Enlightenment? No, we do not; and for two reasons. In the first place, as we have seen, the ancestral Methodism which Kipling inherited, even if he had been far more constantly aware of it than he was (he was baptized in the Church of England), would not of itself give him entry into what we have called "Dissent." And in the second place the Alexander Pope who wrote *Essay on Man* may be, and almost certainly is, an author of the Enlightenment, but the Pope who wrote "Ode on Solitude" and was to write "Imitations of Horace" can be much less confidently placed in that category. Pope was uncomfortable in his age, and at odds with it; in his Horatian poems he is straining against the historical currents that we call "the Enlightenment," which his younger contemporary James Thomson was content and eager to be whirled along by. Moreover, Horace after all is a pagan author; pre-Christian as Kipling, at least after 1918, may be thought post-Christian. Horace's urbanely saturnine disenchantment, which Kipling after so many centuries recovers, is even further from the sanguine and expansive temper of the Enlightenment at its most infidel than it is from the more temperate and sober aspirations of the Enlightenment that remained Christian. One sees very clearly how wrong it would be to identify "the Enlightenment" with "neoclassicism."

Thus we must conclude that on the evidence of our poetry the re-wedding of Dissenting "Revelation" with Enlightenment "Reason" is as far away as ever it was. Another of Browning's heirs in poetry, the American Ezra Pound, was raised a Presbyterian in Philadelphia, but seems to have taken it no more seriously than Kipling took whatever episcopalian or nonepiscopalian Christianity he was exposed to. (As has been noted, Kipling's Freemasonry, which he linked with Mithraism, seems to have been the focus for such religious apprehensions as he had.) And Ezra Pound, to be sure, valued the Enlightenment and was drawn to it, not just as a system of ideas but more momentously as a governing metaphor; but for him it was specifically a *French* phenomenon, and when his comrade T. S. Eliot directed him to Johnson's *Vanity of Human Wishes*, Pound showed himself (in *Guide to Kulchur*) conspicuously less enthusiastic about it than Eliot was. The American Enlightenment of Jefferson and Adams, which Pound deserves much credit for taking seriously when others didn't, is accordingly for him a distinctly French-influenced and therefore infidel phenomenon. And so we look in vain in Pound for any acknowledgment of those poets — Thomson and Gray, Goldsmith and Smart — whom we have taken as the great voices of an *English* Enlightenment. Thus none of Browning's heirs in poetry, precisely because they *were* Browning's heirs, have been able to put together that homogeneous worldview, at once "cultured" and Christian, which Browning's mother may have inhabited in the London suburb of Camberwell about 1820.

And yet . . . "What do they know of England who only England know?" This famous verse — which, so Kipling tells us, was first formulated by his mother — gives us Kipling's imperialism in its pristine, innocent state, before events in South Africa and his own notoriety as semi-official spokesman led him to encase it in increasingly implausible and unpleasing propositions about the Providential election of some races of mankind before others. And in this, its innocent phase, does it not reach back across two centuries to

James Thomson in *The Seasons*, similarly exhorting his countrymen to attain a more than insular vision? And in the making of the British Empire have we not been told how often the Flag followed the Bible? That British dominion in South Africa, for which the Boer War was fought, was achieved reluctantly and with misgiving as inadequate police and military forces were unwillingly committed to protect the intrepid or foolhardy missionaries who had insisted on moving into Dutch and African territories. Moreover, that missionary impetus for good or ill (and there are anthropologists who will tell us of the "ill") was spearheaded by Dissenters; William Carey, the Baptist shoemaker, was the first of them all. In this way, the Empire was very much originally a Nonconformists' empire; and when, in World War Two, the leader of the Chindits in Burma was a member of the Plymouth Brethren, General Orde Wingate, history rather weirdly brought round its revenges. The White Man's Burden was through many generations, for Briton and American alike, the burden of the Holy Scriptures. This consideration opens up a historical perspective which I confess I find myself daunted by. It has, at any rate, a lot to do with Dissenting Christianity and with Rudyard Kipling, and something to do with "Enlightenment." I leave it to be explored by those who are more energetic, and more intrepid, than I am.

Note

1. See *Post*: "Thoughts on Kipling's 'Recessional'."

Related Pieces

The Language of the
Eighteenth Century Hymn [1]

In a way that neither I nor the sponsors of this seminar could have foreseen, my talk has achieved a surprising topicality. In the London *Daily Telegraph* for February 7th this year (1977) appeared a news item under the headline, "MP 'could do better than Betjeman'." And the story below told of a Tory M.P., a Mr. Nicholas Fairbairn, objecting to the Jubilee Hymn composed by the Poet Laureate Sir John Betjeman and Mr. Malcolm Williamson, Master of the Queen's Music, to celebrate the twenty-fifth anniversary of the accession of Queen Elizabeth II. "It is," said Mr. Fairbairn, "absolutely pathetic. It is the most banal, ninth-rate piece of children's verse. It has none of the mystery of poetry about it." And the bold politician undertook to do better in three hours than Sir John had managed to do in three months. Next day, the newspaper followed up the story under the headline, "My words are for music, says upset Poet Laureate." His verses, said Sir John, were *never* to be considered apart from their music, and through his agent he told the press and the breathless populace: "Hymns are not good poems, nor is 'God Save the Queen'."

For our special purposes I believe we must ignore the Poet Laureate's declared wishes, and briefly consider his verses shorn of the music that will attend or embellish or decently obscure them when the hymn is rendered by sixty thousand schoolchildren next July in Liverpool. They are arranged in five quatrains with a chorus. And here they are, chorus first:

> For our Monarch and her people,
> United yet and free,
> Let the bells from every steeple
> Ring out loud the Jubilee.

In days of disillusion,
However low we've been
To fire us and inspire us
God gave to us our Queen.

She acceded, young and dutiful,
To a much-loved father's throne;
Serene and kind and beautiful,
She holds us as her own.

And twenty-five years later
So sure her reign has been
That our great events are greater
For the presence of our Queen.

Hers the grace the Church has prayed for,
Ours the joy that she is here.
Let the bells do what they're made for!
Ring out thanks both loud and clear.

From that look of dedication
In those eyes profoundly blue
We know her coronation
As a sacrament and true.

I experience in any case a certain embarrassment at reading these loyal verses to an audience of presumably staunch republicans (with a small *r*, of course). And I cannot overcome my embarrassment sufficiently to give you the other text that I have with me — which is to say, the product of Mr. Fairbairn's feverish three hours with the Muse. I cannot forbear, however, informing you that Mr. Fairbairn's afflatus permitted him the daring stroke of addressing his sovereign as "Queen glorious, Queen *frail*," and also as "Queen of the British, so valiant and *vain*." At the height of his transports moreover he addresses her as "Our lassie" — which may have something to do with the fact that Mr. Fairbairn sits for a Scottish constituency. At any rate, this poet's audacity as to epithets — "frail" and "vain" — may give us a clue what to listen for as we hear the hymn of the past with which Sir John Betjeman explicitly challenges comparison — that is to say, "God Save the Queen," the national anthem, which is (he tells us) as far from being "a good poem," as is his own Jubilee Hymn. I give this in the form it had when first printed in full in *The Gentleman's Magazine* for October 1745 under the title, "A Loyal Song, Sung at the Theatres":

> God save great George our King,
> Long live our noble King;
>> God save the King.
> Send him victorious,
> Happy and glorious,
> Long to reign over us;
>> God save the King.

> O Lord our God arise,
> Scatter his enemies,
>> And make them fall.
> Confound their politicks,
> Frustrate their knavish tricks;
> On him our hopes we fix;
>> O, save us all.

> Thy choicest gifts in store
> On George be pleased to pour;
>> Long may he reign.
> May he defend our laws,
> And ever give us cause
> To say with heart and voice,
>> God save the King.

Here the only epithets that are ascribed to the monarch are "great" and "noble" — the latter, I believe, not crediting him with nobility as a moral virtue but asserting only that he is of noble (meaning, exalted) lineage. The other epithets — "victorious," "glorious," and "happy" (that last, I suspect, more in the sense of "lucky" than in our modern sense) — are not ascribed to him, but prayed for on his behalf. And now let me remind you of Sir John Betjeman's epithets for *his* sovereign: she is, he says (or in some cases, she *has been*) "young and dutiful," also "Serene and kind and beautiful," and her eyes are "profoundly blue." Of these epithets the most just and the most affecting, to my mind, is "serene" — which is more affecting, one may think, than any of the attributes given by the poet to her ancestor, George II. Remarkably, serenity is almost the first quality attributed to Her Majesty by the rival poet, Nicholas Fairbairn; and one sees why — to be unflurried, rigorously consistent in her public demeanor, conspicuously removed above the jar and din of partisan policies and ideologies, is required of a twentieth-century monarch far more urgently than of an eighteenth-century one. There is a lot of history in and behind the choice of this word; and that is certainly one of the things that we ask of words in poetry. As for the other epithets . . . "kind"? Well, yes — it is better no doubt to have a kind Queen than an unkind one, though in twentieth century circumstances it is much less important for her to be kind than to be "serene," or to be "dutiful," which last may be regarded as the *sine qua non*. But "beautiful" . . . ? I shall not be so ungallant as to ask if this word is accurate. But it *is* to the point to ask how important it is that the monarch be handsome. And surely we must reply: the comeliness or uncomeliness of a monarch matters hardly at all. As for her being blue-eyed rather than grey-eyed or hazel-eyed, or her being profoundly rather than shallowly blue-eyed . . . to regard this as anything but a sentimental irrelevance would lay one open to charges of *racism,* perhaps.

I hope it is clear that these are serious questions to ask, and that the answers to them have a lot to do with how we judge the *poetic* merit of such verses as these. And my point is a very simple one — that the author of the stanzas to George II took seriously both the monarchical system of government and the divine providence which it assumes as necessary to it. That the head of state be "great" (i.e. with notable powers at his disposal), that he be "victorious" (over foreign enemies), and that he be "glorious" (that last, I take it, comprehending all that the Renaissance meant when it asked that its princes be "magnificent"), above all that the monarch be "happy" (fortunate, blest with good luck) — these are indeed the things to be wished and prayed for, in all seriousness, as his being blue-eyed or hazel-eyed emphatically is not. Sir John Betjeman, though we happen to know that he is both a convinced monarchist and a devout Anglican, is less than serious about these matters in his verses. And thus I believe we may say that the National Anthem may or may not be "a good poem" (I hold that in its modest measure it is), but that certainly it is nearer to that status than is Sir John's Jubilee Hymn, since it passes the first and minimal test of taking seriously what its words say, *each* of those words, severally and together.

How far we can consider it an eighteenth-century hymn is what we may next consider. Certainly it is not what would first spring to our minds as an example of that category. And the extraordinary possibility that it was first composed in French in 1686 by Mme. de Brinon, to music by Lully, and sung to Louis XIV, though this notion was magisterially dismissed eighty or more years ago by the great hymnologist Julian, is still current — as you may satisfy yourselves by consulting *The Sun King* (1966) by the late Nancy Mitford. It is nowadays often ascribed to the obscure and wretched Henry Carey (1687?— 1743), and an eighteenth-century correspondent claimed to have heard it sung by Carey in a Cornhill tavern in 1740, to celebrate Admiral Vernon's defeat of the Spaniards at Portobelo in the Caribbean. But Carey's son didn't claim it for his father until 1795, and accordingly the ascription to Carey has been much disputed. However, just such dubiety is (I suggest) of the nature of the congregational hymn. For the hymn, like the ballad or the folk-lyric, is transmitted to us by oral tradition rather than through the channels of copyright. With eighteenth-century hymns this may seem not to be the case. After all, if in church we are using *Hymns Ancient and Modern* and we are directed to a hymn beginning, "O Thou, before the world began/ Ordained a Sacrifice for man . . . ," we may look to the name at the head or the end in our hymnbook, and find there the name of Charles Wesley. But what appeared over Wesley's name in *Hymns for the Lord's Supper* (1745) was a hymn beginning:

> O Thou Eternal Victim slain,
> A sacrifice for guilty man . . .

which is a great deal more disconcerting. And in 1745 the second stanza ran:

> Thy Offering still continues new,
> The vesture keeps its bloody hue,
> Thou stand'st the ever-slaughter'd Lamb,
> Thy Priesthood still remains the same,
> Thy years, O god, can never fail,
> Thy goodness is unchangeable . . .

whereas *Hymns Ancient and Modern* has huddled the bloody purchase out of sight, and gives us, for "The vesture keeps its bloody hue," the inoffensive though ungrammatical "Before the righteous Father's view."

The point is obvious enough, and familiar to all of us: though in the eighteenth century a hymn-writer normally subscribed his name under the hymns he composed, this has never meant — and the author cannot have conceived it *would* mean — what it means in the case of a secular poet. To this day, ministers of religion and choir-masters and even individual worshippers have no compunction about keeping a name like Isaac Watts at the foot of a hymn, even though in singing and often enough in reprinting that composition they habitually leave out certain verses and completely change others. Thus — to stay with the Anglican *Hymns Ancient and Modern* — one of the most famous and popular of Watts's hymns, "When I survey the wond'rous Cross," appears in that hymnbook shorn of its fourth quatrain:

> His dying Crimson like a Robe
> Spread o'er his Body on the Tree,
> Then am I dead to all the Globe,
> And all the Globe is dead to me.

To my mind this omission, by muting the elaboration of the emblematic motif of the Redeemer's blood, emasculates the piece quite grievously. And it has the additional disadvantage of concealing how far Watts, English Dissenter though he was, was happy to emulate the iconography of the Roman Catholic Counter-Reformation, as he had studied it for instance in the Latin poems of "the Christian Horace," the seventeenth-century Polish Jesuit Matthew Casimire Sarbiewski.

The question is what we should do about this. As literary scholars, our first impulse is to protest in outrage, and apply ourselves to reestablishing an exact canon and an uncorrupted text. But I'm not at all sure that we should act on our first impulses. For when a text like this ceases to be "corrupted," it ceases to be alive as a still germinating presence in the ongoing consciousness of the English-speaking peoples. We must beware of stacking away on library shelves a text of which the living place is still in tattered hymnals, on insecure music stands, and in the inexact memories of infrequent worshippers. When a few months ago I was castigating an English audience for consistently ignoring Isaac Watts, and thereby perpetuating the outrageous fiction that eighteenth-century poetry was barren of devotional lyrics, my good friend Professor Frank Kermode argued very forcibly that to instate Watts's hymns and his versions of the psalms as texts for study along with Thomson's *Seasons* and Pope's *Imitations of Horace* would be to do a notable disservice to Watts, and also (more important) to the still not extinguished trains of thought and feeling which Watts preeminently articulated for the English-speaking peoples. (And incidentally, in case the point needs to be made, my use of that expression, "the English-speaking peoples," is deliberate; Watts, like Doddridge and Charles Wesley also, is a continuing presence in the experience of the American people — as witness the extraordinary liberties taken with Watts's texts by American Unitarians at the end of the eighteenth century. And what goes for American culture is true also of for instance Australian, even, I discover with pleasure, of a considerable number of people in the subcontinent of India.) This is a hard pill for the scholarly conscience to swallow — that the selfless devotion of the scholarly editor may be a kiss of death. Yet I think the point is well taken. And this is the reason for insisting that the congregational hymn belongs with anonymous and oral forms of poetry like the ballad. The literary scholar must learn to deal with them as he has learned to deal with the ramifying versions of Child's Border Ballads, where we do not suppose that a relatively late version recorded in the Appalachians or the Ozarks is an inferior because corrupt version of some pristine original which alone, if we can recover it, merits a scholarly *imprimatur.*

At this point it is useful to go back for a moment to my clippings from *The Daily Telegraph,* where we read how the Master of the Queen's Music rallied to help his beleaguered collaborator by declaring that Sir John's words were "deceptively simple," and testifying that "Sir John has simplified and simplified it and has written it specifically to be sung." For it was Isaac Watts who first seemed to insist on simplicity as of the essence of hymn writing. Watts wrote:

> In many of these composures, I have just permitted my verse to rise
> above a flat and indolent style; yet I hope it is every where sup-
> ported above the just contempt of the critics: though I am sensible
> that I have often subdued it below their esteem; because I would
> neither indulge any bold metaphors, nor admit of hard words, nor
> tempt the ignorant worshipper to sing without his understanding.

And in his "Short Essay toward the Improvement of Psalmody,"
Watts is more vehement: "It was hard to sink every line to the level
of a whole congregation, and yet to keep it above contempt." On
the one hand this shows that Watts, in his anxiety to keep his
compositions "above contempt," "above the just contempt of the
critics," certainly did not agree with Sir John Betjeman that "hymns
are not good poems," that the poet who turns to writing hymns
thereupon abandons all his aspirations and scruples as a poet. (And
Watts, it must be said, was making a real sacrifice; for there are
among his *juvenilia* poems which show he was capable of writing in
a very bold and exuberant style.) What is more important, however,
is to recognize that in considering literary style there is no concept
more complicated than "simplicity." Are we after all right to assume that when Watts calls his verse style "flat and indolent" (or
rather, elevated by just one degree above that), he means what we
would mean by "simple"? Or again, when he speaks of his effort
"to sink every line to the level of a whole congregation," did he
mean what the Master of the Queen's Music means when he says
that Sir John "has simplified and simplified it"? Watts and Mr.
Malcolm Williamson *may* be saying the same thing, and again they
may not.

For a test case we may turn to one of Watts's hymns which
enables us, as happens very rarely with him, to glimpse him actually
in the act of composition. For it was amended by Watts after his
first edition had appeared. It is a hymn to which he gave the title,
"The Passion and Exaltation of Christ," and I think it is seldom or
never sung — for reasons which are significant, though not hard to
find. In the first edition it ran like this:

> Thus saith the Ruler of the Skies,
> *Awake my dreadful Sword;*

> *Awake my Wrath, and Smite the Man*
> *That's Fellow to a God.*
>
> Vengeance receiv'd the dread Command,
> And armed down she flys,
> Jesus submits t'his Father's Hand,
> And bows his Head and dies.
>
> But oh! the Wisdom and the Grace
> That join with Vengeance now!
> He dies to save our Guilty Race,
> And yet he rises too.
>
> A Person so divine was he
> Who yielded to be slain,
> That he could give his Soul away,
> And take his Life again.
>
> Live, glorious Lord, and reign on high,
> Let every Nation sing,
> And Angels sound with endless Joy
> The Saviour and the King.

This is one of the pieces by Watts which cannot help but remind us that, despite the accommodating blandness of his demeanor and conduct in Hanoverian London, he was doctrinally as Calvinist as his master Richard Baxter (though not enough, incidentally, to satisfy Jonathan Edwards). It is one of many pieces which, when we remember them, make us boggle at Élie Halévy declaring, of Hanoverian Dissenting ministers like Watts, that "they preached a doctrine more and more like that of Aristotle or Cicero, instead of Christianity according to Saint Paul." We shall have to look a long way in Aristotle or Cicero before we encounter the vengeful God who irrupts into Watts's first stanza, with *"Awake my dreadful Sword;/ Awake my Wrath, and Smite the Man/ That's Fellow to a God."* And for Watts the fearsomeness of a God smiting humankind by smiting not man but the God-Man, Jesus, is, even so, not rammed home forcefully enough. For in later editions the first stanza read:

> Thus said the Ruler of the Skies,
> *Awake my dreadful Sword;*
> *Awake my Wrath, and smite the Man*
> *My fellow,* saith the Lord

The question arises: Is this ferocious emendation in the direction of greater simplicity? And I think we have to say that it is, that the second version seals off any loopholes by which to evade the fearsomeness of what Watts is saying. But if so, the simplicity is as far as possible from what A. E. Housman had in mind forty years ago when, after quoting four lines of Watts, he declared fatuously, "That simple verse, bad rhyme and all, is poetry beyond Pope." On the contrary, where Watts is concerned, what we call "simplicity" is more properly *clarity*. In this poem as a whole the language is made transparent in order that we shall not blink; and what we cannot blink is less the fearsomeness of what he is saying, than its irrationality or (better still) its meta-rationality. What Watts's clarity forces his readers and hearers to confront is the irrationality that is *paradox:* the central paradox of the God-man breeding inevitably the corollary paradoxes by which to die is to rise, and to give the soul away is to take life back. The language is "simplified"; but there is nowhere any simplifying of the content, which is *doctrine,* paradoxical as Christian doctrine necessarily is.

And it is no insult to Sir John Betjeman to deduce that the simplifying which *he* conscientiously pursued can hardly have been of this sort. He was simplifying not just language but doctrine also. For the "doctrine" of monarchy involves, if it is not blasphemous to say so, a paradox of the same sort, if not of the same order, as the paradox of Jesus the God-man. To apprehend the Queen-woman involves a movement of the mind on two levels at once: humanly, Elizabeth is a woman of her time basically like any other, having for instance blue eyes rather than hazel eyes; but emblematically or mythically she is also, and at the same time, the United Kingdom personified. The humble Christians for whom Watts wrote were, he judged, capable of the intellectual and imaginative athletics which this involved; the hearers of the Jubilee Hymn are not, so the Poet Laureate seems to decide. And of course he is prudent to think so, since rationalizing intellectuals through many generations have shown themselves incapable of it.

Watts and Philip Doddridge and the Wesleys were sophisticated and learned men who deliberately purged their language of everything that would make it inaccessible to men and women who were less sophisticated and less learned than they were. And in the process, as they must have realized, they denied themselves the Shakespearean or Popian splendors that depend upon allusion and mysterious resonance and obliquity. They imposed upon themselves the same self-denying ordinance that after them William Wordsworth was to observe when he wrote his *Lyrical Ballads*. And the same is true of William Cowper, at least of the Cowper who wrote religious poems. Yet Cowper stands apart. Although "God moves in a mysterious way" and the still lovelier "Sometimes a light surprises/ The Christian when he sings" are poems by Cowper which have been adopted as greatly cherished hymns, hymnologists have rightly pointed out that they are hymns only with a difference. Indeed, though I have described the eighteenth-century hymns as devotional lyrics, and think that I was right to do so, yet "devotional lyric" fits Cowper's Olney hymns more purely and exactly than any others. For the congregational hymn as we find it in Watts or Wesley or Doddridge or Toplady is necessarily public utterance, whereas "Sometimes a light surprises" is a wistful private musing. Partly the difference is that the other men were ministers, leaders of congregations, where Cowper was merely one of those who sat at their feet. This has the effect that whereas all the other hymns have at their center the exposition of scriptural doctrine (that being indeed what gives them intellectual sinews and verbal precision), at the center of Cowper's hymns is not doctrine, but *experience* — as we recognize when we reflect that as God moves "in his mysterious way," among the "wonders" that he performs is the peculiar fate of intermittent suicidal depression with which he has visited his poet.

In any case, there is at least one outstanding hymn-writer of the eighteenth century who seems to present us with a different language from the purged but still educated and elegant English of the eighteenth-century gentleman. This is John Newton, Cowper's collaborator on the Olney Hymns.[2]

There are few nowadays to whom the Reverend John Newton is even a name. And among those few there are some, I fear, for whom the name conjures up a grotesque image, both comic and horrifying, of a Pecksniffian hypocrite who walked the planks of his slave ship in the Atlantic, reflecting aloud, for the sake of the human cattle chained to their gratings below, "Glorious things of thee are spoken/ Zion, city of our God"; a monster of complacency who later, after a well-publicized "conversion," harried into insanity his parishioner William Cowper, by hellfire sermons expounding Calvinist doctrine at its most rigid and ferocious.

In fact Newton, as the captain of a slave ship, was as humane as possible by the standards, and given the conditions, of the slave trade in his day. His conversion was publicized much later, precisely to give ammunition to those who wanted the slave trade outlawed. The records of the Evangelical Movement show that, far from being an extremist, Newton continually tried to mediate between the Calvinist and the Arminian wings. And as for Cowper, he had known suicidal fits of insane melancholia before he ever met Newton, and the seeds of it were in congenital hypochondria. But all this, it will seem, is to plead no more than mitigating circumstances. By the standards of his day, both in his first profession and his second one, John Newton was temperate and enlightened — very well; but then (it will be said) the standards of his day were abominable. It is better to take the bull by the horns and admit that Newton was a remarkably simple, even an obtuse man. This at least saves him from the charge of hypocrisy. He was sincere within his limits, which were narrow.

Long before humanitarian feeling and the political genius of William Wilberforce made the slave trade a burning issue of social morality, men like James Thomson and William Shenstone had perceived the monstrous anomaly of Sunday services at sea for the crews of slave ships. But Newton, self-educated, represents a much less sophisticated level of society than Thomson or Shenstone or his own friend, Cowper. And for the historian, just that is his irreplaceable value. Newton on his last voyage committed to his diary his fears of an insurrection among his slaves:

> We have not been wanting in care to keep it out of their power, yet (as the best mere human precaution is insufficient to guard against everything) they had found means to provide themselves with knives and other dangerous weapons and were just ripe for mis-

chief. So true it is that except the Lord keep the city the watchman watcheth in vain!

We find it hard to credit a simplicity which could in all good faith subscribe that last pious reflection. Yet it's just this *naiveté* which, later in Newton's life, produced his best hymns:

> The prophet's sons, in times of old,
>   Though to appearance poor,
> Were rich without possessing gold,
>   And honour'd, though obscure.
>
> In peace their daily bread they eat,
>   By honest labour earn'd;
> While daily at Elisha's feet
>   They grace and wisdom learn'd.
>
> The prophet's presence cheer'd their toil,
>   They watch'd the words he spoke,
> Whether they turn'd the furrow'd soil,
>   Or fell'd the spreading oak.
>
> Once, as they listened to his theme,
>   Their conference was stopp'd;
> For one beneath the yielding stream,
>   A borrow'd Axe had dropp'd.
>
> 'Alas! it was not mine,' he said
>   'How shall I make it good?'
> Elisha heard, and when he pray'd,
>   The iron swam like wood.
>
> If God, in such a small affair,
>   A miracle performs,
> It shows his condescending care
>   Of poor unworthy worms.
>
> Though kings and nations in his view
>   Are but as motes and dust,
> His eye and ear are fix'd on you,
>   Who in his mercy trust.
>
> Not one concern of ours is small,
>   If we belong to him;
> To teach us this, the Lord of all
>   Once made the iron swim.

This disconcerting *literalness* in the reading of the Christian Revelation was something that more complex and self-conscious writers like Isaac Watts and George Herbert (they were Newton's favorite poets) strove to attain by strenuous moral and artistic discipline. Those who know Newton from his logs and diaries, from his "Authentic Narrative" (of his own conversion), from his innumerable letters, will realize that for him on the contrary this *naiveté* was natural. The absence of conscious intention and strategy, the lack of pressure and strain behind the ultimate transparency, certainly makes Newton's hymns inferior, as poems, to the poems of Herbert and the best hymns of Watts and Cowper. Yet the product speaks for itself. Its poetic virtues are minimal perhaps, yet real and rare, and moral as much as literary. For it is honesty, the refusal to slip anything over on the reader or the congregation, which pins down the miracle at its most literal, by *rhyme:*

> 'Alas! it was not mine', he said,
>   'How shall I make it good?'
> Elisha heard, and when he pray'd
>   The iron swam like wood.

And it is the same wide-eyed concern to get the point home at its most astounding which justifies what seems at first sight a clear case of that bane of eighteenth-century poetry, the superfluous because "stock" epithet:

> For one beneath the yielding stream
>   A borrow'd axe had dropp'd.

It is of the nature of streams to "yield." This one didn't — and that's just the point; simple enough in all conscience, but in its very simplicity massively disconcerting.

The tang of colloquial idiom is everywhere in Newton:

> The Manna, favour'd Israel's meat,
>   Was gather'd day by day;
> When all the host was serv'd, the heat
>   Melted the rest away.
>
> In vain to hoard it up they try'd,
>   Against tomorrow came;
> It then bred worms and putrify'd,
>   And proved their sin and shame.

'Twas daily bread, and would not keep,
    But must be still renew'd;
Faith should not want a hoard or heap,
    But trust the Lord for food.

The truths by which the soul is fed,
    Must thus be had afresh;
For notions resting in the head
    Will only feed the flesh.

However true, they have no life
    Or unction to impart;
They breed the worms of pride and strife,
    But cannot cheer the heart.

Nor can the best experience past
    The life of faith maintain;
The brightest hope will faint at last,
    Unless supply'd again.

Dear Lord, while we in pray'r are found,
    Do thou the Manna give;
Oh! let it fall on all around,
    That we may eat and live.

"'Twas daily bread, and would not keep . . . ," "Must thus be had afresh . . ." — this is the language of the eighteenth-century small shopkeeper and thrifty housewife, an idiom which has not got into English poetry at all, except through the hymnbook. Perhaps Newton's most audacious and brilliant use of the colloquial is, on an off-rhyme, at the end of "By the poor widow's oil and meal":

Then let not doubts your mind assail,
    Remember God has said,
"The cruse and barrel shall not fail,
    My people shall be fed."

And thus, though faint it often seems,
    He keeps their grace alive;
Supply'd by his refreshing streams,
    Their dying hopes revive.

Though in ourselves we have no stock,
    The Lord is nigh to save;
The door flies open when we knock,
    And 'tis but ask and have.

The people who spoke this language — and John Newton who wrote for them, because he was one of them — are much stranger to us than their social betters whom we encounter in poetry so much more often. They were, for instance, much more callous, in a way which our humanitarianism finds hard to forgive, which is however easy to understand when we consider that they were only one defaulting creditor away from Gin Lane or the Debtor's Prison, only one press-gang away from the floating slums that were the British warships. They had, in any case, compensating virtues. In particular they saw piety and religious observance in terms of history which was literally true, and doctrine that was to be explained, and then accepted or rejected, not explained away or allowed to dissolve behind a mist of emotional indulgence. At their most fervent, their fervor was always related to the literally true and the doctrinally exact. As a result they produced a body of religious poetry which is the least *religiose* of any that one can think of.

Notes

1. This address was first delivered at the William Andrews Clark Memorial Library, Los Angeles, on 5th March, 1977. It has been published, along with a lecture by Robert Stevenson on "The Eighteenth-Century Hymn Tune," as *English Hymnology in the Eighteenth Century* (Los Angeles, 1980).

2. From this point to the end of my paper, I reproduce verbatim what I wrote on pp. 24–29 of my anthology, *Augustan Lyric* (London: Heineman Educational Books, 1974).

An Episode in the History of Candor[1]

I believe I can supply a footnote, or perhaps several footnotes, to a document already a quarter-century old, William Empson's *The Structure of Complex Words* (1951). In chapter 15 of this book Empson considered the semantic history of two English words, "sensible" and "candid." Respecting the latter he was intrigued by an exchange in Jane Austen's *Pride and Prejudice:*

> "I would wish not to be hasty in censuring any one; but I always speak as I think."
>
> "I know you do; and it is *that* which makes the wonder. With *your* good sense, to be so honestly blind to the follies and nonsense of others! Affectation of candour is common enough — one meets it everywhere. But to be candid without affection or design — to take the good of everyone's character and make it still better, and say nothing of the bad — belongs to you alone."

Empson remarks of this, very justly:

> Jane Austen's use of the word here . . . is very far from the unquestioning use which could assert an equation in the word as normal. It examines rather sceptically just what kind of truth-telling is involved, and the result is a definition. . . . A candid person picks out the good points in a person's character and ignores the bad ones. . . .

In other words, in the 1790s, if one were in any way scrupulous and alert and honest as a speaker or writer of English, one had to recognize that "candor" and "candid" were suspect words, very problematical.

Even a few years before, this had not been the case. Dr. Johnson had defined "candor" in his *Dictionary* as "Freedom from malice,

favourable disposition, kindliness; 'sweetness of temper, kindness'."
And in the Preface to his Shakespeare (1765) he uses the term firmly
and without qualification, as if usage had not yet distorted or
perverted it. Thus, of those who had quarrelled with Warburton's
annotations to Shakespeare Johnson writes:

> Let me however do them justice. One is a wit, and one a scholar.
> They have both shown acuteness sufficient in the discovery of
> faults, and have both advanced some probable interpretations of
> obscure passages; but when they aspire to conjecture and emenda-
> tion, it appears how falsely we all estimate our own abilities, and
> the little which they have been able to perform might have taught
> them more candour to the endeavours of others.

And here we need to pause.

For "candor" and "candid," like some other words in our language, have so changed in meaning that their current meaning, now
in the twentieth century, can seem to be one hundred and eighty
degrees away from the meaning that they had two hundred years
ago. Nowadays, when an acquaintance begins, "To speak candidly
. . . ," we brace ourselves; because we know that what he will go on
to say, about a third person or more probably about ourselves, is
something disparaging: "I think you were wrong . . ."; or, "I think
you behaved rather badly . . ." In the eighteenth century, as
Johnson's definition and his usage makes clear, the expectation was
precisely the opposite: "To speak candidly . . ." introduced a statement of the order of, "Though he may seem to have behaved badly,
I believe he meant well"; or, "You are not so much in the wrong as
you think." In the eighteenth century a *candid* person was one who
habitually gave others the benefit of the doubt, who thought the best
of others until he was compelled to think worse. In this sense,
"candor" was for the eighteenth century the name of a very lofty
virtue indeed — equivalent indeed to the virtue of Christian *charity*.
And in fact, in 1768 the biblical scholar Edward Harwood, translating the First Epistle to the Corinthians, translated "charity" by
"candor," when for "Charity beareth all things, believeth all things,
hopeth all things, endureth all things," he wrote of "Benevolence"
that it "throws a vail of candour over all things." This is very plain
from another sentence from Johnson's Preface to Shakespeare,

where he says of previous commentators, "They have all been treated by me with candour, which they have not been careful of observing to one another . . ."; and then goes on to say, "It is not easy to discover from what cause the acrimony of a scholiast can naturally proceed."

The puzzle of course, for us as for Empson, is to understand why inside thirty years "candor" and "candid," such firm and respectable words for Doctor Johnson, had become such besmirched and questionable words as they clearly were for Jane Austen. The *N.E.D.* gives an example from 1798 which Empson took note of, from George Canning's "New Morality" in the *Anti-Jacobin*:

> "Much may be said on both sides," hark, I hear
> A well-known voice that murmurs in my ear, —
> The voice of Candour. Hail! most solemn sage,
> Thou drivelling virtue of this moral age,
> Candour — which softens party's headlong rage;
> Candour — which spares its foes; nor e'er descends
> With bigot zeal to combat for its friends.
> Candour — which loves in see-saw strain to tell
> Of acting foolishly, but meaning well;
> Too nice to praise by wholesale, or to blame,
> Convinced that all men's motives are the same;
> And finds, with keen discriminating sight,
> Black's not too black, nor white so very white . . .
>
> Give me the avow'd, th'erect, the manly foe.
> Bold I can meet — perhaps may turn his blow;
> But of all plagues, good Heav'n, thy wrath can send,
> Save, save, oh! save me from the Candid Friend!

William Empson commented with honest puzzlement:

> One would suppose that the Victorian fear of outspokenness was the strongest enemy of the grace of the word, and it is hard to invent a reason why the song should appear as early as 1798. Perhaps it is part of the feeling that the Augustan settlement had become artificial; the word presumes a code of manners which had become vulgarised, and the attack on it is a sort of minor parallel to the attack on Poetic Diction.

Rather plainly, both of the explanations that Empson here offers are snatched at desperately; he doesn't believe in either of them himself — and for good reason. For the Victorians, as we know, were a great deal more outspoken on some things than we can afford to be — for instance, on whether, in order to be a Christian, you have to believe in the Holy Trinity. And as for "the Augustan settlement," it had split in two a full thirty years before, when Goldsmith and Johnson took arms against Thomas Gray and his imitators. A historical explanation that is worth anything must come up with something better than this.

And the explanation, I think, is quite near at hand — though in a place where we're not likely to look; in David Bogue's and James Bennett's *History of Dissenters from the Revolution in 1688, to the Year 1808*. In this work, published in 1810, Bogue and Bennett advise their readers:

> The misapplication of the word candour was more injurious in its effects on religious sentiments, than can now be well conceived. It was supposed to possess indescribable virtues. Candour was sounded from many a pulpit; and like charity, it was supposed to hide a multitude of sins. An orthodox minister who had candour was to believe that an arian or socinian was a very good man; and that if he was sincere in his opinions, and not rigid in condemning others, he ought not to be condemned himself. The influence of this idea was exceedingly pernicious; for it led to an indifference with respect to truth and error, which depraved both their sentiments and dispositions, which relaxed the springs of Christian integrity and conduct, and gradually brought them to call good evil and evil good, to put light for darkness and darkness for light. This was another of the arian idols. Dr. Doddridge, whose softness of temper led him to more intercourse with ministers of the new opinions than most of his brethren, was sensible of the blindness of this boasted candour, and frequently mentions, with considerable feeling, that its possessors could exercise it to all but those who were the ardent believers of evangelical doctrine. (*op. cit.* p. 384)

This suggests that "candor" and "candid," in the firm Johnsonian sense, were casualties of the Evangelical Movement which (it might be argued, though not very plausibly) in the second half of the eighteenth century brought back heat and asperity into theological controversy.

However, this is still too broad to be satisfactory. "The Evangelical Movement" is not much better than "the Augustan settlement." The quarry that we are seeking ought to be, and it can be, pinned down more precisely. Most of the clues are in the sentences just quoted. But unfortunately they are such clues as we nowadays are unable or unwilling to decipher; for not only are "Arian" and "Socinian" words that few of us can define, they belong in a field of discourse that we are impatient with. Do they not point, for most of us, to worries and troubles that we are happy to think have long ago "blown over"? Can we not be content to say that in the eighteenth as in other centuries the acrimony of theologians destroyed Christian charity itself, and brought both that and a related principle like candor into disrepute? We shall be the readier to think so, if what faces us as an alternative is not just plunging into eighteenth-century theology, but into (as appears) the theology of eighteenth-century *Nonconformists*! For even among stalwart Nonconformists of our own day (who are not easy to find, incidentally) the eighteenth century is commonly held to be a sterile interval between the ardors and exaltations of Milton and Bunyan in the century before, and the more dubious fervors and fanaticisms of the nineteenth century that follows. And as for the rest of us, it is hardly too much to say that we find it hard to remember or to conceive how in the eighteenth century there were any Nonconformists at all. How far, and in what way, when we speak of "the Augustan settlement," do we conceive of that settlement as comprehending an heir of John Bunyan such as Philip Doddridge? It is very seldom, I fear, that we even raise the question. And yet what was called "the Dissenting Interest" was a powerful political reality that no eighteenth-century politician could ever afford to ignore.

Political considerations are something we shall have to return to, for the *Anti-Jacobin* has already shown us that we must. It is the political implication of candor, or of false candor, that Canning is striking at in his verses of 1798. But for the moment what is more necessary is to understand just what an important matter we are dealing with. When we are examining the disintegration of a moral principle so firm and so central as candor was for a man as good as Dr. Johnson, we are doing a great deal more than filling in a missing chapter of semantic history; we are dealing with the collapse of a civilization, or of one of its crucial pillars. And to the great name of Johnson I believe we may add two others not less great; Berkeley and Swift. For I have argued elsewhere that for both of these unsparing and critical minds from the early years of the century, candor was a moral principle as important as it was for Johnson later. (See my "Berkeley and the Style of Dialogue," in *The English Mind*, 1964.) If, to understand what happened to candor, we need to go into the squabbles of the dissenting sects, it is something we should be ready to do for the sake of any one of these great Anglicans. And it is worth saying, by the way, that so far as I can understand these three men, each of them would have known just what he meant by terms like "Arian" or "Socinian," would have regarded them as words of very ill omen, and would not have thought he wasted his time in opposing the ideas which those words stand for.

Squabbles of the dissenting sects . . . But when we look, we discover to our surprise that in the eighteenth century the dissenting sects squabbled among themselves hardly at all. The Dissenting Interest held together, monolithic; the three sects — Baptist, Presbyterian, and Independent (that is, Congregationalist) — made common cause, and recognized a common interest, to the extent indeed that a dissenting minister over his preaching career could wander across the sectarian lines and serve in turn a Baptist, a Presbyterian, and an Independent flock. One not untypical case from the end of the century is the once famous John Clayton (1754 – 1843), who incidentally in the 1790s was a firm and eloquent Tory. (It is widely believed that no Dissenters supported William Pitt and the war against France; but John Clayton was not the only dissenting minister who did so.) One of Clayton's admirers, challenged to say what denomination his pastor belonged to, replied: "I have heard that he is considered to be an *Independent Presbyterian Methodist*" — and here the only oddity is the "Methodist," for of course Methodism did not become an independent sect at all, until the eighteenth century was out. Clayton's Victorian biographer (T. W. Aveling, *Memorials of the Clayton Family*, 1867) remarks, "This is a description which sounds strangely, and was never before heard of. . . ." And his puzzlement is natural; for the nineteenth century

saw each of the dissenting sects — including many that now appeared for the first time, like the Plymouth Brethren, and the
various sorts of Methodism — draw its skirts ever more fastidiously
away from those which in the previous century had been its dissenting brethren. And the reason for this is what brings us back to the
Congregationalists Bogue and Bennett, and to their angry denuncia-
tion of "this boasted candour."

For the eighteenth century saw the dissolution and collapse from
within of one of the three ancient dissenting communions — of just
that one of them, indeed, which at the beginning of the century
(remember Dryden's *The Hind and the Panther*) had seemed the
strongest of all. This was the English Presbyterian church, which by
1800 survived only in name, and in 1813 lost even that. For 1813 was
the year in which Parliament recognized Unitarians as Dissenters
on a par with any others; and this only acknowledged the virtually
complete takeover by the Unitarians of what had once been English
Presbyterianism. Indeed, not only had the Unitarians thus taken
over one-third of "the Dissenting Interest," they had come within
an ace of taking over, or at least of dominating, the remaining two
churches also. This was in 1772, when an appeal was made to
Parliament for the repeal of the Toleration Act of 1688 — an
obscure episode, yet in its way a crucial one for English history
generally, not just for English Dissent. For the appeal was drawn up
by Unitarians masquerading as Presbyterians, and those of the
Thirty-Nine Articles from which they sought to be excused were
those that asserted the dogma of the Trinity. Yet this was a dogma
which the majority of English Dissenters, good Calvinists as they
were, recognized as freely and fervently as ever the Anglicans did.
Thus the Unitarians, by claiming to speak for the Dissenting Interest as a whole, were pretending to speak for a Trinitarian majority
though in fact they spoke only for an anti-Trinitarian minority,
themselves. The Calvinist majority woke up only just in time; and it
was they, the provincial Dissenters, who ensured that the appeal
failed when it was brought in a second time, in the session of 1773.
The consequences however were very damaging; for it had revealed
to the Establishment that the Dissenting Interest was disunited, and
so the Establishment was emboldened, in 1790, to resist the far

juster claim for the repeal of the Test Act. And it is this conspicuously "uncandid" maneuver by the Unitarians that is in the angry
minds of the Trinitarians Bogue and Bennett when they link false
candor with Arianism and Socinianism, those being the anti-
Trinitarian heresies which the Unitarians espoused. It was to prevent a recurrence of such successful infiltration that nineteenth
century Dissenters jealously insisted on their denominational and
sectarian peculiarities; it was to prevent heretics like the Unitarians
from ever again disguising themselves under an ancient and honored and orthodox name like "Presbyterian." And the crucial point
is that "candor" was indeed the slogan inscribed on the banner
under which the Unitarians deviously fought in 1772 and 1773. The
historian of the episode, Anthony Lincoln (*Some Social and Political
Ideas of English Dissent, 1760 − 1800*), is being far more ironical than
he realizes, when he decides that the application of 1772, for the
repeal of the Toleration Act, "as a whole, was sincerely what it
professed to be: an appeal to 'candour'." And if support is needed
for this interpretation of what was in Bogue's and Bennett's minds,
one may turn to their Baptist contemporary, Joseph Ivimey in 1823
(*History of the English Baptists*, Volume 3, p. 400n.), commenting that a
Baptist congregation in the eighteenth century was led to accept the
Socinian James Foster as their pastor by, he says, "their false
notions of candour and catholicism."

Now, this is not the view of these matters which is commonly
received. By the Whig and the Marxist interpretations of history
alike, it is assumed that "toleration" is a good thing, which one
cannot have too much of. It falls by default to the historian of
language to protest that nomenclature is being abused when a
name — like "Christian," or like "democrat" — is tolerantly ex-
tended to cover people who in fact deny one of the cardinal dogmas
by which "Christianity" or "democracy" is defined. Let us be
tolerant indeed, let tolerance be unconfined; but let us at the same
time call things by their right names! It was by failing to obey this
rule, by for instance calling "Presbyterian" what was in fact
"Unitarian," that our ancestors seem to have brought "candor" and
"candid" into disrepute, and thus lost the moral principle that
meant so much to Berkeley and Swift and Johnson.

As for David Bogue and James Bennett and Joseph Ivimey — they were I'm afraid obscurantist bigots, the three of them. And they bequeathed their obscurantism and their bigotry to succeeding generations — a woeful legacy which both the Congregationalist and the Baptist communions labored under through most of the nineteenth century. But some of the blame for that must lie with their liberal and professedly Presbyterian brethren who hoodwinked and outmaneuvered them, until they recoiled (too late) into this sullen ferocity. Doddridge's enlightenment and liberality — in a word, his *candor* — had, they thought, served only to deliver him into the hands of the Arian false friends who were his enemies; if that was what enlightenment and liberality brought about, then enlightened and liberal were things that no Dissenter could afford to be. And so we find Bogue and Bennett declaring elsewhere, with unmistakable satisfaction: "The reading of Dissenters themselves, is very much limited to religious books; for being neither men of leisure nor of wealth, few of them go beyond their favourite hallowed circle. The frequency of preaching among them, and of devotional meetings, leaves them little opportunity, or desire, for a more extensive range" (*op. cit.* p. 306). It was what Philip Doddridge would not have wanted to say of the Dissenters of the 1740s, nor would it have been true of them.

We are now in a position to understand the *Anti-Jacobin* in 1798, furious at

> Thou drivelling virtue of this moral age,
> Candour — which softens party's headlong rage;
> Candour — which spares its foes; nor e'er descends
> With bigot zeal to combat for its friends.

In one way of course, this shift to a political implication for "candor" and "candid" does not need to be explained. For historians of the Left, like Edward Thompson in *The Making of the English Working Class*, constantly remind us that the Arians and Unitarians of the 1770s and 1780s — Joseph Priestley, Richard Price, Gilbert Wakefield, Robert Robinson — were also the pro-French democrats of the 1790s. They were "liberal" in the one sphere as in the other, and appealed to "the candid reader" on the one set of topics as on the other. What Canning registers, however, is a phenomenon which some of us can remember as recurring almost exactly one hundred and fifty years later: the "liberal" whose candor consists in thinking the best about the postrevolutionary state abroad, and the worst about his own nonrevolutionary state at home; giving the benefit of the doubt to France or to the Soviet Union, while never giving any benefit at all to the United Kingdom or the U.S.A. And of course this character is still with us, though except among surviving Stalinists and Trade Union leaders, the foreign state for which he exercises his candor is no longer the Soviet Union. Indeed this figure is so familiar an actor on the political scene, now as in 1951 when Empson was writing, that it's surprising we should have any difficulty understanding what Canning is driving at.

But the answer surely is what we have seen already. "Liberalism" is thought to be a good thing, of which we cannot have too much; and so we conspire not to notice when liberalism in religion takes us out of religion altogether, or when liberalism in politics leads us to condone the denial of political liberties to ninety-nine citizens out of every hundred. It is these muddles and duplicities, with which we are thoroughly familiar, that are in the mind of Jane Austen when she finds "candid" and "candor" such treacherous words.

All the same, there is a new inflection to the words in Canning's lines.

> Candour — which loves in see-saw strain to tell
> Of acting foolishly, but meaning well;

. . . yes, this fits well enough the Western liberal who apologizes for communism. But what of the next lines? —

> Too nice to praise by wholesale, or to blame,
> Convinced that all men's motives are the same;
> And finds, with keen discriminating sight,
> Black's not too black, nor white so very white . . .

Does not this picture of the timid temporizer fit a different political animal altogether? Not really. The date is 1798; that is, it belongs to the period of *The God That Failed*. By 1798, all but the inflexibly prejudiced or obtuse could see that revolutionary France had become Bonapartist France, a military dictatorship, just as by 1951 all but the stupid and the bigoted could see that revolutionary Russia had become the dictatorship of Joseph Stalin. And the ho-hum-much-to-be-said-on-both-sides attitude is what false candor, "liberalism," is forced to when it has been thus belied by irrefutable events.

Note

1. This essay first appeared in *PN Review* 4 (1977), pp. 46 – 49.

A Day with the DNB[1]

When the forty-niners of California, lacking yeast, wanted to bake
their sourdough bread, they had need of a "starter," a fermenting
agent — in their case, warm raw milk and flour — which, suitably
tended and occasionally refreshed, would preserve and regenerate
itself indefinitely through a series of later bakings. In the same way,
properly to savor the delights of the *DNB*, one needs a *starter*, in the
shape of a sentence bringing together a number of more or less
obscure names, attached to long dead people who are asserted to
have something in common. Once the process of speculative fer-
mentation is thus started, it can and does renew itself indefinitely
out of the resources of *DNB* itself — as we shall see. But the initial
provocation must be there, or must be supplied.

For the purposes of this day's representative entertainment, I
have taken a sentence from a recent book by the Reader in History
at the University of Edinburgh, H. T. Dickinson, his *Liberty and
Property: Political Ideology in Eighteenth-Century Britain* (1977). The
sentence reads (it is on p. 202): "Those who campaigned most
vigorously for religious toleration and especially for the repeal of
the Test and Corporation Acts were often also at the forefront of
the movement for political reform." Nothing there, to ferment or
germinate! But the sentence is keyed to an end-note (p. 342), and
that gives us what we are looking for:

> Dissenters who campaigned for both religious toleration and politi-
> cal reform include Richard Price, Joseph Priestley, Thomas Paine,
> John Cartwright, William Godwin, James Burgh, John Disney, Mary
> Wollstonecraft, Capel Lofft, David Williams, Andrew Kippis,
> Thomas Brand Hollis, Joseph Towers, Thomas Walker, George
> Dyer and William Enfield. . . .

Such riches! The true devotee or addict of *DNB* is already intoxicated — sixteen names, some not wholly unfamiliar, others wholly so, which can now, this initial provocation registered, be explored one by one in purring contentment through the double-columned pages of the many volumes. Each of the articles now to be perused can be trusted to provide other names with the happy adjunct "*q.v.*"; masters of Cambridge colleges, Bishops of Carlisle, self-educated Dorsetshire printers and compilers, others, more than enough to sustain bemused pedantry through days and indeed weeks of browsing. But we are restricted to one day; we must remember that.

And so . . . First, Richard Price (1723 – 91): "His father, Rice Price, who was for many years minister of a congregation of protestant dissenters at Bridgend . . . was a bigoted Calvinist, and seems to have been a person of morose temper, facts which may account, on the principle of reaction, for the liberal opinions and the benevolent disposition of the son." Blessedly pre-Freudian *DNB*, which has discerned, without nudgings from Vienna, that sons often set out to be all that their fathers were not . . . But wait! Richard Price, it appears, was like Rice (or Rhys) Price, "minister of a congregation of protestant dissenters," not at Bridgend indeed, but in the London suburb of Newington Green. However "both Price and Priestley" (Priestley is to come up next, and we are agog) "were in theological opinion what would now vaguely be called 'unitarians'; in 1791 Price became an original member of the Unitarian Society. But Price's opinions would seem to have been rather Arian than Socinian." Though we may well for good or ill be as "vague" about Unitarians as were the first subscribers to *DNB*, and wholly in the dark about the difference between "Arian" and "Socinian," still the crucial point comes over — that Richard Price was, though still somehow Christian, satisfyingly far from the "morose" and "bigoted" Christianity of his papa. This must be part of what is meant by crediting him with "liberal opinions"; though we soon find that he was "liberal" in ways and in fields where we may feel more at home — it seems that he wrote pamphlets in favor of both the American and the French revolutions. Accordingly, "Dr. Johnson naturally placed Price in the same category with Horne Tooke, John

Wilkes and Dr. Priestley, and resolutely refused to meet him; Gibbon compared him to the 'wild visionaries' who formed the 'constituent assembly' of 1789." "Naturally"? Well yes, *naturally*; who does not know that Dr. Johnson, though a great and good man, must be thought in politics neither great nor good, holding to political sentiments that were not on the side of the future? We must certainly think so, if we are to sympathize when the *DNB* biographer (he is Thomas Fowler) remarks, "The darker side of the Revolution Price happily did not live to see. . . . On 19 April 1791 he died, worn out with suffering and disease. . . ." For Edward Gibbon, it seems clear (and perhaps Dr. Johnson also), might have reflected unsympathetically that for Price not to foresee "the darker side of the Revolution" suggests some deficiency in him as a political thinker. But plainly this is not a reflection invited by Thomas Fowler, who goes on to tell us that "his funeral was conducted at Bunhill Fields by Dr. Kippis, and his funeral sermon by Dr. Priestley, names which, like his own, are specially honorable in the roll of English nonconformist divines."

That the name of Joseph Priestley is "specially honorable," nobody should want to deny. What may surprise us is the "roll" on which his honored name is said to be inscribed; for "experimental scientists" and "political libertarians" are rolls on which we might expect to find this name entered, sooner than in the category, "nonconformist divines." *DNB* (Philip Joseph Hartog) does indeed tell us that as early as 1755 Priestley was "presbyterian minister at Needham Market, Suffolk," and that "the London presbyterians helped him by the usual subsidy from their fund, and by occasional benefactions through George Benson . . . and Andrew Kippis. . . ." And yet how can this be, since we have already learned from the article on Price that Priestley no less than Price was what we would nowadays call ("vaguely") Unitarian? Hartog himself tells us that "though his preaching was uncontroversial, he made no secret of his Arianism, which alienated some hearers." In the 1750s and presumably subsequent decades in England, did "Unitarian" and "Presbyterian" amount to the same thing? There is a puzzle here, which we may hope that subsequent researches will elucidate.

Meanwhile we note that, like Price, Priestley was bought up on strictly Calvinist doctrine, which he rejected.

And Andrew Kippis, that other "specially honorable name" which has already cropped up in both the articles we have so far consulted? Ah, the further we probe, the more we shall find that cropping up is very much what Andrew Kippis (1725 – 95) was good at. He is defined as "nonconformist divine and biographer." As "biographer" Kippis must have been of special interest to *DNB* writers (like Thompson Cooper, who writes this article), because *Biographia Britannica*, on which Kippis labored with Joseph Towers (*q.v.* — he is another on our list) was an aborted pilot-project for what *DNB* itself was to become more than a century later. Of Kippis's and Towers' second edition of *Biographia Britannica*, of which five volumes appeared between 1778 and 1793 (ending in the middle of entries under "F"), Thompson Cooper judges that it "hardly deserves the high praise which has been sometimes bestowed upon it. . . . Many of the new memoirs were of inordinate length, and the prominence given to nonconformists laid the editor open to a charge of partiality." One would like to know (what for that matter someone may have established) whether the *DNB* compilers could resist profiting from Kippis's earlier labors, and whether accordingly the charge of partiality to Nonconformists may not be brought against *DNB* itself. If that should be so, Kippis's services to his fellow sectaries would be all the more effective for being so self-effacing. Dr. Johnson told Boswell that he (Johnson) had had the chance of undertaking this second edition; and that he regretted having refused the commission — one can imagine why, from Boswell's own complaint (later withdrawn however) that *Biographia Britannica* was "too crowded with obscure dissenting teachers." Plainly, no dissenting teachers were going to stay "obscure" if Andrew Kippis could help it. And he was one of them: educated under Doddridge at Northampton, thereafter a dissenting pastor at Dorking (1750 – 53), and (for 43 years!) at Westminster, Kippis combined his pastoral cares with tutoring in the Coward Academy at Hoxton, and from 1786 in the radical new Dissenting Academy at Hoxton, where his pupils included William Godwin and the poet Samuel Rogers. He also wrote many books, including a *Life of Captain Cook* (1788). Oh a very busy man was Andrew Kippis, with a finger in every dissenting pie! And what released that multifarious energy was the same with him as with Price and Priestley: "When about fourteen years old he renounced the principles of Calvinism, in which his relatives had brought him up. . . . Subsequently he inclined to Socinianism. . . ." And then — oh blessed *DNB*! — Thompson Cooper blows the gaff on Kippis and Price and Priestley and many others on our list. For he quotes Wilson's *History of Dissenting Churches* to the effect that Kippis "highly disapproved the conduct of the modern Socinians, in assuming to themselves the exclusive appellation of unitarians." This is the giveaway. We need look no further to explain the nominal Presbyterianism of Joseph Priestley, and the equally nominal denominational allegiances of others on our list. Unitarian wolves in Calvinist sheep's clothing! Astute Andrew Kippis — his shrewd advice was widely followed; and so not just in *DNB* but by historians since, including our own H. T. Dickinson, "Nonconformist" or "Dissenter," as applied to Englishmen of the later eighteenth century, means almost invariably "Unitarian."

Mr. Dickinson offers his study (Introduction, p. 2) as an attempt "to meet the challenge of Sir Lewis Namier and his disciples who have laboured so long and so effectively to prove that the ideas and principles of eighteenth-century politicians were merely rationalizations of selfish ambition and base motives." And in order that we shall think more kindly of our ancestors, he claims (ibid., p. 9) that his more sunny conclusions "rest upon the treatises of all the major political thinkers and propagandists, the reported parliamentary debates for 1688 to 1800, and a study of thousands of pamphlets . . . , dozens of newspapers and periodicals, and many works of imaginative literature." And indeed it is evident that he has travelled extensively and doggedly in the sahara of pamphlet literature. It is the more surprising that we look in vain in his Index for any entry for John Martin, Job Orton, John Clayton, or Thomas Sheraton — indeed, for any of the pamphleteering Dissenters who at the time of the American and the French Revolutions espoused a "loyalist" position, and who were pointedly *not* "at the forefront of the movement for political reform." This suggests — how can we avoid the embarrassing suggestion? — a certain political prejudice on the part of our historian.

What is not so clear, and to most will seem less important, is a hint of *sectarian* prejudice also. For Martin and Sheraton were Baptists, as Orton and Clayton were Independents; whereas, if we continue checking in *DNB*, we find that of Mr. Dickinson's list of sixteen "Dissenters" not one is Baptist, and not one is Independent. In other words, of the three ancient communions of orthodox Dissent, only one — the Presbyterian — is represented on his list; and we've already found evidence that through the decades in question Presbyterianism was often a transparent disguise for something quite different, theologically not orthodox at all.

Instead of John Martin and Job Orton, John Clayton and Thomas Sheraton, we are offered . . . Tom Paine! And surely we boggle. If writing *The Age of Reason* isn't enough to move a man outside the Christian communion altogether, then it's hard to conceive what any man can do or say that will not, at a pinch, be gathered under the skirts of "Dissent." What Leslie Stephen says of Paine in *DNB* is that "the father . . . was a member of the Society of Friends, who had a small meeting-house at Thetford. The mother belonged to the Church of England . . ."; and that "Paine's father was registered as a quaker at his death, and the son, as he often avows, was much influenced by quaker principles." Thus it appears that all one has to do to qualify as a Dissenter, in Mr. Dickinson's elastic understanding of the term, is to have one parent who belonged to a dissenting communion, and thereafter, whatever militant infidelity one may promote, to "often avow" that one was influenced by that parent's principles. Only a little less flagrantly, another historian, Caroline Robbins, can label Priestley "Independent," because that was the communion he was born to, which he speedily departed from.

Moreover it appears that one can be at one and the same time a member of the Established Church, and a dissenter from that Church. Thomas Walker for one, who is not in *DNB*, is presumably the same commemorated by Frida Knight in *The Strange Case of Thomas Walker* (1957), where however this radical Manchester merchant, active in the 1790s, is represented as an Anglican. And Capel

Lofft (1751 – 1824) must have been at least nominally an Anglican; otherwise he could not have been educated at Eton and Peterhouse. Undoubtedly this wealthy Suffolk landowner was, as *DNB* says, "a strong whig," devoted to Charles James Fox and indeed to Napoleon, who said "qu'il compterait toujours M. Capell Lofft parmi ses amis les plus affectionnés." He opposed the American war, and advocated parliamentary reform, besides deserving well of all lovers of our poetry by getting into print Robert Bloomfield's *Farmer's Boy* (1798). And of course research since *DNB* may have shown that he at some point joined a dissenting communion; but if so Herbert Ashton Holden, his *DNB* biographer, knew nothing of it.

Another son of Peterhouse was John Disney D.D. (1746 – 1816), whose life is perhaps more entertaining and instructive than any other to which Dickinson's list introduces us. "His grandfather," we learn, "was rector of St. Mary's, Nottingham, but his remoter ancestors were zealous nonconformists." However, this ancestral zeal did not prevent Disney, as soon as he was ordained in 1768, from accepting an honorary chaplaincy from Edmund Law, Master of Peterhouse and Bishop of Carlisle. (Law gets a *q.v.,* but we must restrain ourselves — "In his philosophical opinions he was an ardent disciple of Locke, in politics he was a whig, and as a churchman he represented the most latitudinarian position of the day.") Disney's chaplaincy, we may suspect, did not take him often, nor perhaps ever, to Carlisle. "In 1769 he was presented to the living of Swinderby, Lincolnshire, and soon after to the rectory of Panton, in another part of the same county; he held both livings, residing at Swinderby." He was an active member of the association formed in 1771 to petition Parliament for relief of the clergy from subscription to those of the Thirty-Nine Articles which required belief in the Holy Trinity. When this petition was rejected, Disney did not follow his friend Theophilus Lindsey, most principled of Unitarians, who thereupon honorably resigned his benefice. Like many other Unitarians in Anglican orders, Disney preferred to operate as a "mole" or a "sleeper," as an agent "in place." And not until 1782 did he throw up his preferments, to become the first secretary of a Unitarian Society for Promoting the Knowledge of the Scriptures. In 1793 he took over from Lindsey pastoral duties at the Unitarian

Essex Street church, and he also, as we might have guessed, contributed to Kippis's *Biographia Britannica*. But then — wait for it! — he came into a legacy, and from another of the men named on our list, Thomas Brand Hollis. Thomas Hollis, benefactor of Harvard, duly commemorated in Harvard Yard, a wealthy and restive freethinking radical who died in 1774 (himself often called a Dissenter, for no better reason than that he had Baptist forebears), had left his Dorsetshire estates to his friend Thomas Brand of the Hyde, near Ingatestone, Essex, who took the name of Hollis. And "T. Brand Hollis (d. 2 Sept., 1804) by will dated 1792 left both estates, worth about £5,000 a year, to Disney, who resigned his ministry on 25 March 1805, on the ground of ill-health. . . ." Fancy that! Despite his ill-health Disney lingered for another eleven years, spending them (we are not surprised to learn) "in literary leisure." Alexander Gordon, who wrote the *DNB* biography, says of the period when Disney was still a priest of the Established Church: "Like some others, Disney accommodated the public service to suit his special views. The Athanasian Creed he had always ignored; he now omitted the Nicene Creed and the Litany, and made other changes in reading the common prayer." Oh, a fortunate man was John Disney, and of very liberal views! What a long and happy life was his! It's clear that these early Unitarians, whether they originated in church or in chapel, attentively promoted each other's welfare; but surely none of them profited more than Disney. And how gratifying for him, in his literary leisure in Essex, to know that he had been since 1780 a member of the Nottinghamshire county committee for retrenchment and parliamentary reform; and hence that he was sure of a posthumous reputation as libertarian and democrat!

John Cartwright (1740— 1824) — the famous Major Cartwright of Mark Rutherford's *Revolution in Tanner's Lane* — was a man of very different mettle, though it's not clear how he merits the title of "Dissenter," for *DNB* tells us nothing of his denominational persuasion, nor indeed of his religious sentiments. He could have been an atheist, for all *DNB* tells us. His biographer, Edward Smith, writes charmingly: "Cartwright was one of the most generous-minded public men of his time. He was tender to his opponents, forgiving to detractors, and always open-handed. He saved persons from drowning, at the risk of his own life, on four separate occasions. His writings are excessively dry to the ordinary reader, and quite significant of the enthusiast who could be earnest without being inflammatory." In that last sentence Edward Smith is something better than charming, and the deadpan trenchancy which so closely marshals "enthusiast" along with "earnest" and "inflammatory" shows just how good late-Victorian prose can be at times, in the columns of *DNB*. It shows too how the writers for *DNB* did not think themselves disqualified from passing judgment. The most famous example of this is doubtless Leslie Stephen's sudden and savage characterization of William Godwin: "Godwin, constantly sinking into deeper embarrassment, tried to extort money from his son-in-law until Shelley's death, and Shelley did his best to supply the venerable horseleech." "Venerable horseleech"! Such language is intemperate. And yet the truth is that few people will spring to Godwin's defense; and neither libertarians nor Dissenters are eager to own the author of *Political Justice*. But a Dissenter he was, or at least he has a better title than most of the others on our list. Born the son of a dissenting (in fact, Sandemanian) minister, Godwin in 1773 entered the Hoxton Academy where (wouldn't we know it?) "he was under Kippis, who became a useful friend." After ministering to Dissenters in Ware, in Stowmarket, and in Beaconsfield, "in 1785 he was appointed, through Kippis's introduction, to write the historical article in the 'New Annual Register'. He now dropped the title of 'reverend' and henceforth saw little of his family. . . ." Much later, about 1800, "he was," says Leslie Stephen, "becoming known to Wordsworth, Lamb and Coleridge. To Coleridge's influence he attributes a return to a sufficiently vague theism, having been, he says, converted to unbelief by his conversations with Holcroft about 1787, and having become an atheist about 1792, that is, during the composition of the 'Political Justice'." Plainly, if the rule is "once a Dissenter, always a Dissenter" (and that seems to be the rule that Mr. Dickinson plays by), Godwin, despite his declared atheism, is at least nearer to being a Dissenter than Tom Paine is.

There remain from the list five men (Burgh, Williams, Towers, Dyer, and Enfield) and the one woman, Mary Wollstonecraft — who figures in *DNB* (alas for Women's Lib!) under her married

name of "Godwin." Burgh and Towers and Enfield are not very
interesting: James Burgh (1714 – 75) seems to have been a Scottish
Presbyterian — that's to say, he wasn't a Dissenter so long as he
stayed in Scotland, but technically became one as soon as he
crossed the border; Joseph Towers (1737 – 99), collaborator with
the ubiquitous Kippis, became an Arian — which is to say, almost
certainly, Unitarian — sometime between 1754 and 1764, and from
1774 onwards was "pastor of the presbyterian congregation in
Southwood Lane, Highgate"; and William Enfield (1741 – 97),
though he called himself Presbyterian, must have been Unitarian
likewise, since he was tutor at the Warrington Academy (1770 – 85),
and thereafter minister at the Octagon Chapel, Norwich — both
Unitarian institutions.

The Welshman David Williams (1738 – 1816) is a far more sub-
stantial character, more interesting and deserving of more respect.
His father was "a Calvinist in religion" who "on his death bed made
him promise to enter Carmarthen Academy to qualify as a dissenting minister." He duly studied there, as exhibitioner from the
London Presbyterian Board, which however already suspected that
academy of disseminating Arian and Arminian principles. From
1758 Williams was a dissenting minister in Frome, and from 1761 to
1769 in Exeter, but left both churches because he preached a
theology too "liberal" for his congregations. Later, in 1773 and 1774,
he published proposals for the instituting of a nondenominational
chapel in London, and these were, says his *DNB* biographer, "so
deistic in tone as to put an end to the scheme." Williams's relations
with Garrick and Franklin, his activities as educationalist and historian of Monmouthshire, are all interesting, but not to the present
purpose. His *Letters on Political Liberty* (published anonymously, 1782)
are quoted by H. T. Dickinson, as is his *Letter to the Body of the
Protestant Dissenting Ministers of all Denominations* (1777). He went to
France about August 1792, "was made a French citizen, and remained till the execution . . . of Louis XVI, a measure which he
strongly deprecated." Shortly thereafter he returned to London,
bearing secret communications from the French government for
the British ministers, and after the Peace of Amiens (1802) is
thought to have acted as secret emissary in the other direction. Not

unnaturally he incurred "political odium" because of his French sympathies. Williams's deism seems to have impelled him even further from Revelation than the Unitarians like his early patron John Jebb, and it is said to have shocked even such a lax freethinker as Franklin. But at least Williams, alike in his religious and political capacities, frankly put himself in danger, and acted rather than merely opinionating; and he left one monument which survives to this day — the Royal Literary Fund, which he founded.

The poet George Dyer (1755 – 1841) is known as a comically eccentric zany to readers of Lamb's essays, of Crabb Robinson's diaries, and of E. V. Lucas's *Life* of Lamb. His Cambridge college was Emmanuel, where the Master, who showed much interest in Dyer, was a very different proposition from Edmund Law of Peterhouse. He was Richard Farmer (1735 – 97), High Tory and friend of Doctor Johnson. The article on him by Thompson Cooper (for of course I am sneaking a *q.v.*) is very amusing: " . . . his only work of any importance is the 'Essay on the Learning of Shake-speare.' Invincible indolence prevented him from achieving other literary triumphs. He was content to be the hero of a coterie, and to reign supreme in a college combination-room amid the delights of the pipe and the bottle." Farmer's concern for Dyer did not suffice to steer the latter out of the orbit of the Cambridge firebrand Robert Robinson, who could well have figured on H. T. Dickinson's list and would have brought to it one name that was, at least nominally, Baptist. It was Robinson who "led him to unitarianism"; and Dyer's *Memoirs of . . . Robert Robinson* (1796), a book that was owned by Wordsworth, is one of those curious and instructive biographies which damn their subject while intending to vindicate him. H. T. Dickinson quotes from Dyer's *Complaints of the Poor People of England* (1793). And another of Dyer's books provides us with a *q.v.* which we can't afford not to pursue, because it reminds us, if we need reminding, that not everything we turn up out of *DNB* can be dealt with in the spirit of comedy. In 1794 Dyer published an *Account of New South Wales and State of the Convicts . . . with . . . Character of Thomas Fysche Palmer . . .* And the name of Fysche (or Fyshe) Palmer should make us pause and reflect that these Unitarians and Jacobins (or "strong whigs") were playing with fire — a fire which, when stoked by war-fever and the exasperation of the British Ministry, could consume certain unfortunates. Palmer was educated at Eton and Queens' College, Cambridge, "with the purpose of taking orders in the Church of England." Made fellow of Queens' in 1781, Palmer served as curate at Leatherhead, and during this time met and dined with Johnson, as reported by Boswell. "About this time," says his *DNB* biographer Alexander Hastie Millar, "the writings of Dr. Priestley of Birmingham, advocating progressive unitarianism, so strongly influenced Palmer that he decided to abandon the creed in which he had been reared, and to renounce the brilliant prospects of church preferment that were open to him." He served thereafter as Unitarian minister in Montrose and Dundee, where in 1793 he was arrested in connection with an allegedly seditious libel that was not his composition. Tried and convicted, Palmer in 1794 was hurriedly transported along with his "fellow-martyrs" Skirving and Muir — this despite protests in the Commons by Fox and Sheridan, and in the Lords by Stanhope and Lauderdale. At the end of 1799 Palmer, his sentence near to expiry, sailed for home in a trading vessel he had bought with others, and after many adventures in the South Pacific died on a Pacific island in 1802. His body was removed from there in 1804 by an American captain, who transported it to Boston, Massachusetts, where it lies to this day. In 1844 a monument was erected in Calton burying-ground, Edinburgh, "to commemorate Palmer, Muir, and their fellow-martyrs in the cause of reform." If any one wants to call Thomas Fyshe Palmer "Dissenter," I suppose no Dissenter will object; for he was certainly a martyr to *something*, poor fellow.

Andrew Kippis enjoined his fellow Socinians, shrewdly and urgently and as it must seem to us cynically, not to declare themselves such by "assuming to themselves the exclusive appellation of Unitarians." Most of his associates seem to have heeded his injunction: nominally Presbyterians or Anglicans, more rarely Independents or Baptists, they cloaked under these labels their true allegiance, which was Unitarian; that is to say, by the principles of the mostly Calvinist persuasions that they affected to adhere to, they were, all of them, heretics. And Kippis's subterfuge was successful not just in his own day but through many succeeding generations, up to and including (quite notably indeed) our own. To the first generation of subscribers to *DNB*, the words "Unitarian," "Arian," and "Socinian" still had *some* meaning, though probably a meaning less precise than for Kippis and his contemporaries a century before; but for the twentieth-century generations the words have rarely had any meaning at all, however indefinite. And this means that Kippis's maneuver now befuddles the issue more effectively than ever. This I take to be the real significance of H. T. Dickinson's grouping, as "Dissenters," a group of people all of whom Orthodox Dissent would have indignantly disowned. And in this Dickinson is merely following common practice: among those who write of late eighteenth-century England, the term "Dissenter" is bandied about boldly and freely; yet what it means, in virtually every instance, is "Unitarian."

For a last very striking instance of this I go to Claire Tomalin, in her *Life and Death of Mary Wollstonecraft* (1974). There is substance to the complaint that, because of unthinking patriarchal prejudice on the part of Leslie Stephen and his collaborators, *DNB* is much less dependable on women than on men. Accordingly I have thought it prudent, as regards Mary Wollstonecraft, to jump over the *DNB* article and proceed instead to Ms. Tomalin's remarkably sprightly and erudite, impassioned and yet judicious biography, from which we learn for instance that Mary Wollstonecraft was born and reared a slumbrous Anglican, and that (*pace* H. T. Dickinson) her Anglicanism she seems never to have formally renounced, not even when she was married to Godwin.

However, nobody would deny that she felt most at home among people who called themselves "Dissenters," at least from the time in the 1780s when she was in Newington Green, close to Richard Price and much under his influence. What is surprising, in a book so sophisticated as Ms. Tomalin's and apparently addressed to sophisticated readers, is the account which she finds it necessary to give, of the milieu in which Mary Wollstonecraft moved at this time:

> It seemed to her far preferable to hope that men might grow less vicious as the circumstances of their lives grew gentler, rather than

accept that women were given an appearance of virtue only by the crack of the whip; and both the example and the stated beliefs of the Dissenters who surrounded her on the Green encouraged her in this optimistic view. Rational Dissenters, or Unitarians, worshipped reason and Locke; they represented the critical and sceptical tradition of protestantism without its black insistence on guilt. They had thrown out the doctrine of the Trinity, the idea of original sin and the concept of eternal punishment, explaining them all as purely poetic myths. James Burgh's book *The Dignity of Human Nature* breathed the spirit of prudent optimism in which they were inclined to view this world and the next.

Among Claire Tomalin's readers there must surely have been a few who wondered if, after one had "thrown out" the doctrines of the Trinity, of Original Sin, and of Punishment, one had the right to subscribe one's self Christian at all, however "dissenting." The same readers might have recalled that, forty or fifty years earlier, the Calvinistic Independents Isaac Watts and Philip Doddridge had "worshipped reason and Locke" as fervently as Richard Price or James Burgh did, without finding themselves impelled thereby to deny either the Holy Trinity or Original Sin. And, wondering what beyond a rhetorical flourish is involved in calling "insistence on guilt" "black," these readers might recall that to this day Original Sin is a required dogma; and that in the weeks before Christmas the Anglican faithful are still exhorted to meditate on "the four last things" — Death, Sin, Hell, and Judgment. This may or may not be deplorable; but it is a fact.

If these sentences suggest that whereas Claire Tomalin plainly expected her readers to be keen and knowledgeable on most matters, on theology and church history she couldn't expect them to be either, our suspicions are astonishingly confirmed by a footnote she found it necessary to append to her phrase about "black insistence on guilt":

> This particular brand of nonconformity was something quite distinct from Methodism, of which Price thoroughly disapproved, describing it as a faith that ascribed to 'particular feelings, without reason, a supernatural suggestion.'

Well, but *of course*! Who on earth is this reader so ignorant as to need telling that the Methodists, at this time not Nonconformists at all, were at the opposite pole from the Unitarians? I fear the reader in question is too common, as Claire Tomalin recognized by supplying him with this necessary and betraying footnote. But conceivably even in *his* mind the question arises: what of the Dissenters who persisted and worshipped between the extremes of the Methodists on the one hand, the Unitarians on the other? Of them, and of loyalist Dissenters like Orton and Martin, Clayton and Sheraton, we hear no more from Claire Tomalin than from H. T. Dickinson; and throughout the later pages of *The Life and Death of Mary Wollstonecraft*, "Dissenter" means "Unitarian," where it does not mean downright "infidel."

And in these speculations have we wandered too far from considering simply the fun that we can have with *DNB*? By no means! That "fun" certainly comprehends the sardonic amusement that we get, from observing an expedient subterfuge successfully bemusing generations of later historians, including our own. It is, to be sure, a sour and spiteful sort of fun; but who ever thought that sourness and spite are not among the legitimate pleasures of pedantry?

Note

1. This essay first appeared in *PN Review 18* (1980), pp. 26 – 30.

Dissenters and "Antiquity"

In the Preface to his earliest work, the puzzling and ironical
Vindication of Natural Society (1756), Edmund Burke explained that
"the design was to show that . . . the same engines which were
employed for the destruction of religion, might be employed with
equal success for the subversion of government." This seems to
have been a conviction that he never lost. And doubtless we should
bear it in mind when we find him saying, more than thirty years
later, in his *Reflections on the Revolution in France*:

> So tenacious are we of the old ecclesiastical modes and fashions of
> institution, that very little alteration has been made in them since
> the fourteenth or fifteenth century; adhering in this particular, as in
> all things else, to our old settled maxim, never entirely nor at once
> to depart from antiquity. We found these old institutions, on the
> whole, favourable to morality and discipline; and we thought they
> were susceptible of amendment, without altering the ground. We
> thought that they were capable of receiving and meliorating, and
> above all of preserving, the accessions of science and literature, as
> the order of Providence should successively produce them. And
> after all, with this Gothic and monkish education (for such it is in
> the ground-work) we may put in our claim to as ample and early a
> share in all the improvements in science, in arts, and in literature,
> which have illuminated and adorned the modern world, as any
> other nation in Europe; we think one main cause of this improve-
> ment was our not despising the patrimony of knowledge which was
> left us by our forefathers.

The last sentence here shows Burke claiming for himself, and for
the sorts of Englishmen that he claimed to speak for, an "ample and
early" share in the Enlightenment. And indeed how can the claim be
denied to the author of the *Philosophical Inquiry into the Origin of our*

Ideas of the Sublime and Beautiful? But it needs to be remembered when, elsewhere in the *Reflections*, he sarcastically calls "enlightened" Richard Price and the French and English Jacobins. These too could and did lay claim to a share in the Enlightenment; and their claim too should be recognized, but not to the exclusion of Burke and their other adversaries.

However, this is only incidental to the main thrust of Burke's argument. And that argument is uncompromising. One may think for instance that one has heard something similar from John Adams, but this is not so; this is an argument that we do not find, and could not expect to find, in an American like Adams. Although in other respects Burke's attitudes and Adams's are indeed strikingly similar, at this point they part company. For Burke antiquity is *a value in itself*, as it had been for Andrew Marvell when he spoke of the realm of England as "the Great Work of Time"; whereas for Adams, devoted though he was to the common law of England and therefore eager to argue from precedents, antiquity as such, in and for itself, was no argument. At one point in the *Reflections* Burke acknowledges the sort of lawyer's arguments that Adams sets store by, arguments based on constitutional lawyers like Blackstone and Coke and Bracton tracing English liberties to the Great Charter and the Anglo-Saxon kings; Burke acknowledges this line of argument, and shows himself well disposed to it, at the same time that he makes clear it is not *his* argument. For him custom and usage, if they are ancient, are as compelling as precedents established in courts of law. If only because Tom Paine attacked Burke first and Adams later, this difference between them is easy to miss. Yet it is very significant because, despite attempts by modern American conservatives to co-opt Burke for their cause, this difference between Burke and Adams is the crucial difference between English conservatism (when it knows what it is doing, which is seldom) and American conservatism.

We cannot help noticing that in this passage Burke very consciously and deliberately appeals to *pre-Reformation* precedents. And by thrusting at his readers the words "Gothic" and "monkish," he anticipates and by implication sets aside the hostile reactions of antipapist prejudice. Such prejudice was rife among the Dissenters of Burke's day, but it was rife too in the Church of England. And on the other hand there was no reason why Burke's propositions should stick in a Dissenter's craw any more than in an Anglican's. For all the churches of Orthodox Dissent claimed lineage from an antiquity far more remote than the Reformation, precisely because the Reformers themselves had made the same claim. That learned and thoughtful Nonconformist Bernard Manning wrote of the Reformers:

> They did not abandon the past and claim to start a new age. That had often been done. The very form of the Christian doctrine of the Godhead made it easy. Ardent souls confronting an awkward situation set out world history in this manner. God reveals Himself (they said) by degrees. There was an age of the Father, the age of the Old Testament. It ended at the Incarnation. Then came more light: God was known in his Son. That was the age of the New Testament, the Church, the written Word, the Sacraments. But this revelation needs completing; and a third age, the age of the Holy Ghost, will follow. . . . [But the Reformers] did not conceive that the age of the Son had ended or that a new age of the Holy Ghost was to begin. They rejected any doctrine of development which would put in the second place the historic revelation of God in Christ, incarnate in Judaea, recorded in Holy Scripture, represented in the Sacraments. . . . The Reformers did not doubt that the Holy Ghost was in the Church, and that He would lead it into all truth; but they found it the characteristic action of the Holy Ghost to take the things of Christ, not to supersede them.[1]

If I understand the doctrines of "further light" and of "the two covenants," Dissenters who espoused either of these positions (Isaac Backus was among them) could not hold by the Reformers' beliefs, as Bernard Manning here expounds them. But any Dissenter who *did* hold by them could properly claim for his beliefs and practices an antiquity equal to that of any other branch of the Christian Church. And in fact of course, more remarkably, a Baptist justifies his distinctive practice of believer's baptism on the grounds that he is thus keeping faith with the pristine practice of the Primitive Church. In other words, though believer's baptism can be justified on other grounds also, one argument for it is precisely the Burkean argument that sheer antiquity, antiquity as such, carries authority. So it may well seem that English Baptists of the late eighteenth century ought in logic to have been Burkeans, instead of Painites or Priestleyites; and perhaps many more of them were so, than is now acknowledged.

Accordingly it is melancholy but proper to choose, as an example of how many English Dissenters of Burke's day thought far otherwise, one who was at least nominally a Baptist, the bizarre Robert Robinson. This is how Robinson, in his *Ecclesiastical Researches*, treats St. Augustine of Hippo:

> From this bitter and bloody fanatic of Africa, proceeded two hundred and thirty-two pamphlets, an innumerable multitude of epistles, expositions of the gospel, and the psalter, besides sermons, or homilies; and by this man's writings, did Luther, Oecolampadius, and other reformers expound the scripture, and frame an ecclesiastical constitution, to lead Europe into purity of faith and manners; as if Punic faith, and African manners, execrable at Rome when Rome was pagan, were fit for ages enlightened by philosophy and religion. Instead of improving by all the great men that have lived in the last two thousand years, should the world continue to be the disciples of Austin, and his spiritual sense of scripture? He understood the ten commandments in a spiritual sense, and "thou shalt not kill" signified, "thou shalt not kill an orthodox believer." The command did not protect the life of an heretic. This man and his maxims blasted the character of christianity, and excited in the minds of many of the most liberal of mankind just suspicions of the divinity of the religion of Jesus; for the christianity that Austin taught was the scourge and curse of the empire. If Jesus employed him, as he affirmed, to teach occult grace and penal sanctions, for not believing with, and even against evidence; the shame retreats from the obedient disciple, Austin, and revolves on his master, Jesus: but far, very far from every heart be such a thought! It is impossible to defend both Jesus, and Austin, and justice requires the sacrifice of the latter.[2]

A modern reader of this reverend gentleman is likely to throw at him first the accusation "Racist!" And very justly — in a letter of 1786 Robinson writes of "that impudent debauchee, Saint Augustine" as "the man who invented original sin," and concludes his diatribe by calling him "a true Carthaginian, and one of the best examples of Punic faith that ever lived." What we are likely to take less notice of, and be less shocked by, is Robinson's unargued assumption about the relation between Revelation and the unfolding process of recorded history. Plainly, he rejects or denies the conviction of the Reformers as glossed by Bernard Manning, their finding it "the characteristic action of the Holy Ghost to take the things of Christ, not to supersede them." Insofar as they acted on this conviction, by taking over the insights of Saint Augustine, Robinson condemns them. We are often told of the "complacency" of the English eighteenth century; but we are usually asked to discern this complacency in the Tories of the time, whereas it is radicals like Robinson who are surest about "ages enlightened by philosophy and religion." Indeed it is surely obvious that in any age it is the conservatives, wary of departing from precedents embodying the wisdom of the forefathers, who are least complacent about the advances achieved by themselves and their contemporaries, or by what figures as "the modern" at any stage of history.

Tom Paine, accurately discerning just this arrogant and shortsighted complacency in many English Dissenters of his time, made a deliberate play for their allegiance. Thus in a footnote to his *Rights of Man* we read:

> When in any country we see extraordinary circumstances taking place, they naturally lead any man who has a talent for observation and investigation, to inquire into causes. The manufactures of Manchester, Birmingham and Sheffield, are the principal manufactures in England. From whence did this arise? A little observation will explain the case.
>
> The principal, and the generality of the inhabitants of those places, are not of what is called in England, *the Church established by law*; and they, or their fathers (for it is within but a few years) withdrew from the persecution of the chartered towns, where test-laws more particularly operate, and established a sort of asylum for themselves in those places. It was the only asylum that then offered, for the rest of Europe was worse.
>
> But the case is now changing. France and America bid all comers welcome, and initiate them in all the rights of citizenship. Policy and interest, therefore will, but perhaps too late, dictate in England what reason and justice could not. These manufactures are withdrawing, and are arising in other places. There is now (1791) erect-

ing at Passy, three miles from Paris, a large cotton mill, and several are already erected in America. Soon after the rejecting the bill for repealing the test-law, one of the richest manufacturers in England said in my hearing, "England, Sir, is not a country for a Dissenter to live in — we must go to France."

These are truths, and it is doing justice to both parties to tell them. It is chiefly the Dissenters who have carried English manufactures to the height they are now at, and the same men have it in their power to carry them away; . . .

It is not easy to think of a minatory prophecy that was sooner, or more comprehensively, belied in the event. Burke's prophecy, and John Adams's, were on the other hand immediately borne out — by the Terror in France, and thereafter the military dictatorship there. No wonder that Paine's animus against Adams exploded some years later!

In an interesting essay on a neglected topic, Matthew Hodgart has made a case for Paine by contrasting his literary style to that of another radical, the lapsed Sandemanian William Godwin, in his *Political Justice*. Both of them, Hodgart argues, even as they strenuously opposed what Burke had said, learned from his way of saying it. To be sure, Burke's influence combined with others in the forming of Paine's style; though the list that Hodgart gives of those influences and models conspicuously omits the one that Burke himself singled out — "Junius".[3] However that may be, Hodgart is surely right to contend that the cadences of Burke's prose resound in Paine's writing at other times than when he is deliberately parodying Burke's manner, as he was when he turned Burke's rhetoric back upon itself in the famous judgment that Burke "pities the plumage and forgets the dying bird." There is also for instance the justly remembered phrase, "the summer soldier and the sunshine patriot." Paine in fact was a notable phrase-maker, in no derogatory sense. As for Burke's influence on him, and on Godwin also, one must begin by recognizing, as all respectable commentators do, that Burke has not one style, but several — even in the compass of a single work like the *Reflections*. And Hodgart's argument is that whereas Godwin took over from Burke one of his styles that had only limited usefulness, Paine adopted and adapted another that had more color, more vivacity, and was able to deal with a wider range of human and communal experience. "Paine's radicalism," Hodgart says, "like Burke's, is practical, concerned with current issues but also rooted in history — history that includes both the narrative of recent events (in which Paine excels) and the account of the developing constitution of England (in which he is less adept)." In Godwin on the other hand we find an "extreme debility of description and imagery." And this springs from his "almost total rejection of the real worlds of history and of nature":

> He quotes Burke on the miseries of history only to prove that we can learn nothing from history except that it is miserable; it is only what man *can become* when he transcends history that matters . . . we are to think only of the future . . . The body of experience which sustains Burke's and Paine's mature styles is to Godwin not only trivial but somehow vulgar.

Thus the effect, and presumably the intention, of Hodgart's essay is clear; he means to deflect Burke's charge that Paine was a mere "speculatist," by showing how much more this is true of Godwin. And in the course of doing so he has slipped in, or slipped over on us, the description of Burke as himself "a radical." In one way this is plainly just; Burke in the *Reflections*, and still more in the works he went on to write in his last years, is clearly a man almost beside himself with the vision that he has of just what is at issue in the French Revolution. Tory and Whig alike were embarrassed by the fervor of his denunciations and his professions, as right thinking conservatives habitually are by radicals of the Right. But in another sense — the sense that etymology gives us, of "radical" as meaning "root-and-branch" — how can "radical" be predicated of a man so devoted as Burke was to "antiquity," and the authority of antique precedent? And conversely, how can root-and-branch radicalism such as Paine's be reconciled with any respect for antiquity, or even with any historical perspective except the shortest?

In this way Matthew Hodgart's case is ultimately unconvincing. And his concession — that Paine was "less adept" in his account of the developing constitution of England — turns out to fall disingenuously short of the truth. Burke for instance had said in the

Reflections: "The first thing that struck me in the calling the States-General, was a great departure from the ancient course". . . . Paine in a footnote to the *Rights of Man*, quoting this, commented: "And with regard to the 'departure' from the ancient 'course', besides the natural weakness of the remark, it shows that he is unacquainted with circumstances. The departure was necessary, from the experience had upon it, that the ancient course was a bad one." The betraying thing here is the parenthesis, "besides the natural weakness of the remark" — which is in itself enough to show how far Paine was from responding to, positively from *experiencing*, what Andrew Marvell pointed to as "the Great Work of Time." Or again, when Paine jeers at Burke, "he still had not boldness enough to bring up William of Normandy and say, *there is the head of the list! there is the fountain of honour!* the son of a prostitute, and the plunderer of the English nation," Paine either is, or pretends to be, ignorant that for conservatives the legitimacy of monarchical succession derives not at all from *origins*, but from long continuance, precisely from *succession*. Even Robert Filmer in his seventeenth-century *Patriarcha* had admitted that "by the secret will of God many set first do most unjustly obtain the exercise" of supreme power. It ought to be plain that Tom Paine on William of Normandy is as irrelevant, and as raucous, as Robert Robinson on Augustine of Hippo.

And what is the moral of all this for English Dissenters at the present day? No doubt many morals could, and should, be drawn. But one of the most obvious has to do with the Establishment of the Church of England. However unjust and dubious that Establishment may have been in its origins, it has now persisted for long enough to take on the authority of antiquity. As Bernard Manning wrote fifty years ago:

> Many Free Churchmen have no feeling for the Church of England as a national institution, though they cherish it as a part of Christ's Church; but not a few Free Churchmen like myself . . . have a tender regard for the Church of England as it now stands as a national institution, while we shrink with some horror from the thought of its being turned into a disestablished, self-governing episcopalian sect.[4]

So different are most modern Dissenters, from those whose allegiance Burke rightly spurned in 1790.

However, Bernard Manning's "tender regard" in not often reciprocated. Twice already in this essay I have alluded to Marvell's "Horatian Ode upon Cromwell's Return from Ireland":

> 'Tis madness to resist or blame
> The force of angry Heaven's flame;
> And if we would speak true,
> Much to the man is due,
>
> Who, from his private gardens, where
> He lived reservèd and austere
> (As if his highest plot
> To plant the bergamot),
>
> Could by industrious valour climb
> To ruin the Great Work of Time,
> And cast the Kingdom old
> Into another mould.

It is no doubt found as hilarious on the Conservative as on the Labour benches of the present House of Commons that certain political thinkers of a conservative cast, such as Roger Scruton and C. H. Sisson, have found in themselves sufficient reverence for antiquity to make of this three hundred and thirty-year-old poem a cornerstone in their understanding of the realm of England, and how it works. For instance, in Sisson's *The Spirit of British Administration* (1959) "the great work of time" crowns, in so many words, a most eloquent and cogent passage (pp. 156–7) on how the Crown, the continuity and majesty of it, is crucially necessary to a British administrator's understanding of what he is doing. Unfortunately, to an Anglican constitutionalist like Sisson the perception of this "great work of time" is possible, it appears, only to members of the Church of England — as becomes deplorably explicit in a later book, *The Case of Walter Bagehot* (1972). And thus by Sisson, very much as by Matthew Arnold a century ago, the English Dissenters are parcelled together and — without their having any say in the matter — consigned in a lump to the rancorous and contumacious Left.

And the Left, grateful for this unsolicited gift (which brings with

it after all electoral as well as ideological advantages), uses it sometimes astutely, always impudently, and sometimes in ways that are
weird and wonderful. In the 1930s for instance Bernard Manning's
civil and temperate voice had no chance of being heard against John
Maynard Keynes in *The New Statesman and Nation*:

> . . . the post-war generation of intellectual Communists under
> thirty-five. Them, too, I like and respect. Perhaps in their feelings
> and instincts they are the nearest thing we now have to the typical
> nervous nonconformist English gentlemen who went to the
> Crusades, made the Reformation, fought the Great Rebellion, won
> us our civil and religious liberties, and humanised the working
> classes last century.[5]

Here certainly we have an appeal to English antiquity — though to
one that was never heard of before. Even readers of *The New
Statesman and Nation* under Kingsley Martin (himself lapsed from
ancestrally Dissenting stock, as was Keynes also) must have sup-
pressed a start of surprise at the information that the
Nonconformist sects were in existence at the time of the Crusades;
some may have wondered whether "nervous" was to be understood
to mean "jumpy" or in its archaic sense of "sinewy"; and if any of
"the working classes" had by 1939 graduated to the readership of
Mr. Martin's magazine so strenuously dedicated to their interests,
such readers may have resented the implication that they could not
be and were not "humanised" until the gentry, Nonconformist or
not, performed the necessary surgery upon them.

Not all professions of common cause between the British Left
and English Dissent are so entertaining. Little amusement can be
wrung for instance out of the standard practice by which leaders of
the Labour Party, when they want to minimize revolutionary
Marxism among their rank and file, tell the nation soothingly that
either Nonconformity or Methodism (it is never clear which, nor
does it matter) has contributed more than Karl Marx to the Labour
Party's ethos and ideology.

And nowadays this arcane marriage between Dissent and the
Left is sometimes offered to us in versions that are not comical at
all, but touching. Such is for instance the version given by Edward

Thompson. This is affecting because what Thompson understands as "Old Dissent" is a home that he has built for himself after having been driven out of, or else having relinquished, the doctrinaire Marxism which had harbored him, in and out of the Communist Party, through many decades. As he writes himself, at a painful moment early in his "Open Letter to Leszek Kolakowski":

> To be a British Communist, on this empirical island anchored off Europe, was never a matter of great international relevance. . . . But to be a Communist dissident or revisionist, or a relict of that tradition, in 1973, is to be a null quantity like a foreign postage-stamp twice cancelled, unusable and not worth a collector's attention.[6]

For the author of *The Making of the English Working Class* (1964) thus to present himself as a relict, an anachronistic survivor, is at first sight astonishing. For in recent years has any work remotely comparable been more admired, more widely disseminated, and (we have reason to suppose) more influential? It turns out however that in that book, as still a Marxist, Thompson broke through to an erstwhile unpersuaded and large public at precisely the time when he was being disowned by the guardians of the Marxist scriptures. Of this Thompson's open letter to Kolakowski, and the entire volume called *The Poverty of Theory*, leave us in no doubt: they rehearse more than once, and in a tone one can describe only as "wounded," a story of how Thompson and a few who thought like him were, from 1962 onwards, gradually but inexorably dislodged by the British Marxist intelligentsia from positions in which their understanding of the Marxist tradition could carry much or any weight with the Marxist faithful. They reached the unpersuaded precisely when the erstwhile persuaded defected from their persuasion. And so Thompson feels that he has been "shelved" inside the intelligentsia of the British Left — a community, so he persuades us, of positively *familial* intimacy (and subject therefore, as families are, to "flaming rows").

Accordingly it is hard to deny this refugee the refuge which he now seeks, among the English Dissenters. That he does seek it is clear. He tells Kolakowski: "If you are tolerant, you may consider me as a representative of a residual tradition, like Old Dissent, adhering meticulously to old forms whose significance daily diminishes. Like an eighteenth-century Quaker, who will not bare his head before authority nor take oaths, I will not take my holidays in Spain nor attend conferences in Rome funded by the Ford Foundation." And a few sentences later, perhaps playing the pathos for a little more than it is worth, he concedes to Kolakowski: "Operating within a culture of universal rationality you cannot be bothered with the sectarian susceptibilities of another nation's Old Dissent." This tenderness towards Dissent had shown up already in *The Making of the English Working Class*. And indeed Thompson in that book, in order to do justice to the rebellious sectaries of past centuries, was prepared to jettison the patronizing Marxist metaphor of "base" and "superstructure." The abandoning of that mechanical metaphor, so as to assert that the religious liberty which the sectaries fought for was *truly* what they fought for — this is, it appears, the original sin for which the Marxist *apparatchiks* cannot forgive Thompson, or Christopher Hill either. And yet . . . how is it possible to sustain Thompson's claim to belong to "Old Dissent"? Those Old Dissenters were Christians, as Thompson explicitly and vehemently isn't — is it not just as simple as that?

This parting of the ways, which Thompson refuses to recognize, confronted him at an earlier stage in his letter to Kolakowski, at the first point indeed where he is moved to ill temper in his communication with the distinguished Polish defector whom he addresses mostly in sorrow, though sometimes in anger. Kolakowski, declaring himself in *Encounter* an "inconsistent atheist," had decided that "men have no fuller means of self-identification than through religious symbolism," and that "religious consciousness . . . is an irreplaceable part of human culture, man's only attempt to see himself as a whole" — whereat, Thompson avows, "not only the atheist but also some primal Lollard or Anabaptist within me rebels." And this provokes Thompson into what is surely regrettable chauvinism:

> You may say this in Poland: you may say this, if you wish, in Italy or France. But by what right, what study of its traditions and sensibility, may you assume this as a universal in the heart of an ancient

Protestant island, *doggedly resistant to the magics of religious symbolism even when they remained believers*, cultivating like so many urban gardeners the individual conscience as against some priest-given "religious consciousness"?

The italics here are mine — mine, who am no Polish bad or lapsed Roman Catholic but an Englishman bred, unless I am mistaken, much nearer than Edward Thompson to the heart of English Dissenting Protestantism. And what, I ask him, are those "magics of religious symbolism" which those English Protestants were "doggedly resistant to"? Are they for instance, or do they include, that bread or that wine sacramentally offered alike in the Roman Mass, the Anglican Eucharist, and the Dissenters' Lord's Supper? If they do include these, then there is no way in which people who rejected them, as "magics" (an abusive term) or as "symbolism" (a contentious one), could have "remained believers," though they may have deluded themselves that they did. This is true of Lollards and Anabaptists, however "primal." There truly is a point at which Believer and Unbeliever part company; there truly is *not*, as Thompson and many thousands suppose, a continuous band of sentiment and opinion all the way from Belief to Unbelief. Reaching the point where an act of belief is called for, one makes the act or one does not; and one lives with the consequences. If Thompson lives with the consequences of his unbelief, there is no way for him to claim shelter under "Old Dissent."

He fulminates further, to Kolakowski:

What you touch off in me — and this is why I introduced the point — is simply the old Adam of the English idiom. You interrupt me in my work. I don't wish to be dragged back into all *that*, I don't wish to be drawn into an argument whose form and even whose philosophical terms arise from a culture in which the old ding-a-dong between Catholic and atheist universalists goes on and on and on; in which, generation after generation, the Catholic theologians and philosophers, like cunning groundsmen, prepare new pitches and dictate to their opponents that they must, once again, play over every inch of this novel pitch or they will have lost the series; in which, to stand somewhere between Catholic and anti-Catholic philosophy, is to give one a unique status as a Referee.

Thompson's polemical English is here at its vigorous best; and it needs to be, for he hasn't a rational leg to stand on. Just because he is addressing a Pole gives him no warrant for using "Catholic," meaning apparently *"Roman* Catholic," instead of (what the context calls for) "Christian." On the other hand his furious impatience — "You interrupt me in my work" — is wholly understandable, and justified; between Christian and atheist any debate is indeed a waste of time, because they share no common ground. (To be sure, both may justly claim to be "rational"; but they proceed upon incompatible notions of human Reason.) What *isn't* justifiable is Thompson's laying claim to "the old Adam of the English idiom." In other places — notably in his essay, "The Peculiarities of the English" — he has made responsible and in fact heartwarming play with this notion, "the English idiom" (an idiom that comprehends for him, as for few others, the usages of the English poets); but here he implies, quite without warrant, that the English idiom is essentially an *irreligious* idiom, whereas it needs to be asserted bluntly that the English were until lately (and are still, more than any one likes to acknowledge) a Christian nation, and that their idiom comprehends unmistakably Christian deposits, including quite notably usages that an atheist will want to reprehend as "magics" or as "symbols."

All the same, it should be clear why whatever Edward Thompson writes about Dissent deserves from us close and remorseless attention such as we would not give to others. When he speaks of "an ancient Protestant island" we may detect, little as Thompson might like it, the note of Edmund Burke, and Burke's conviction that "antiquity," long continuance, possesses in itself an authority that we should recognize. We do not expect to hear such a locution from a Tory mouth; and if we should hear it, we should be expected to understand by "Protestant" only one version of English Protestantism, that of the Church of England. Other versions are just as ancient as Anglicanism, and have no less authority; though one listens in vain for any acknowledgment of that from the British Right. Angus Calder has linked Thompson's name with a couple of others to stand behind his expostulation:

> People in Britain really must stop conceiving their own history in terms of kings and queens and Regency rakes and Victorian country

houses, and recognise the centrality of those ethical concerns — generating scientific advances, practical action in commerce and industry, missionary-led expansion, reform at home — which were expressed in conventicles, in chapels, in kirks, and in the re-reading of Milton, Bunyan and the Bible. Otherwise we really cannot live with ourselves honestly.[7]

The most fervent of constitutional monarchists should be able to say, "Amen."

Notes

1. Bernard Manning, "The Reformation and the Free Churches" (1938), *Essays in Orthodox Dissent* (1939).

2. George Dyer, *Memoirs of the Life and Writings of Robert Robinson* (1796), pp. 371 – 72.

3. M. J. C. Hodgart, *The English Mind*, ed. H. S. Davies and G. Watson (1964). Hodgart's list of stylistic influences on Paine is cited from H. H. Clark (ed.) *Paine: Representative Selections* (1944, 1961).

4. Bernard Manning, "A Free Churchman's View of an Established Church" (1931), in *Essays in Orthodox Dissent*.

5. *New Statesman and Nation* 28 (January 1939); quoted by Andrew Boyle, *The Fourth Man* (1979: Bantam Books, 1980), p. 160.

6. "An Open Letter to Leszek Kolakowski" (1973), in *The Poverty of Theory* (1978).

7. Angus Calder, in *Proteus*, February 1978.

Thoughts on Kipling's "Recessional"[1]

In an unconsidered moment — or rather in one very ill-considered undertaking, *After Strange Gods,* a book that it seems he was later ashamed of — T. S. Eliot spoke of the Congregationalism that D. H. Lawrence grew up in as "vague hymn-singing pietism." It was an aberration that F. R. Leavis never allowed Eliot, nor the rest of us, to forget. However, years later it may be thought that Eliot more than made up for it, when he wrote appreciatively of another English author, one who stands in almost exactly the same relation to Wesleyan New Dissent that Lawrence stood in to Old Dissent. This author was Rudyard Kipling, grandson of Wesleyan ministers on both sides of his family, whose parents conformed to nonpracticing Anglicanism, and who was himself through much of his life some sort of undogmatic theist. Of Kipling, Eliot wrote in 1941:

> He might almost be called the first citizen of India. And his relation to India determines that about him which is the most important thing about a man, his religious attitude. It is an attitude of comprehensive tolerance. He is not an unbeliever — on the contrary, he can accept all faiths: that of the Moslem, that of the Hindu, that of the Buddhist, Parsee or Jain, even (through the historical imagination) that of Mithra: if his understanding of Christianity is less affectionate, that is due to his Anglo-Saxon background — and no doubt he saw enough in India of clergy such as Mr. Bennett in *Kim.*

This is liberal indeed, and represents (it may be thought) a great increase in Christian charity over the Eliot who wrote *After Strange Gods,* to whom his Anglican allegiance was so much more of a recent and exciting novelty.

However, before we set this change of heart entirely to Eliot's credit, we need to take note of certain difficulties which arise in our reading of the poet for whom he is soliciting our admiration. There is for instance what is probably the most justly famous of all Kipling's poems, his "Recessional" of 1897:

> God of our fathers, known of old,
>   Lord of our far-flung battle-line,
> Beneath whose awful Hand we hold
>   Dominion over palm and pine —
> Lord God of Hosts, be with us yet,
> Lest we forget — lest we forget!
>
> The tumult and the shouting dies;
>   The Captains and the Kings depart:
> Still stands Thine ancient sacrifice,
>   An humble and a contrite heart.
> Lord God of Hosts, be with us yet,
> Lest we forget — lest we forget!
>
> Far-called, our navies melt away;
>   On dune and headland sinks the fire:
> Lo, all our pomp of yesterday
>   Is one with Nineveh and Tyre!
> Judge of the Nations, spare us yet,
> Lest we forget — lest we forget!
>
> If, drunk with sight of power, we loose
>   Wild tongues that have not Thee in awe,
> Such boasting as the Gentiles use,
>   Or lesser breeds without the Law —
> Lord God of Hosts, be with us yet,
> Lest we forget — lest we forget!
>
> For heathen heart that puts her trust
>   In reeking tube and iron shard,
> All valiant dust that builds on dust,
>   And guarding calls not Thee to guard,
> For frantic boast and foolish word —
> Thy mercy on Thy People, Lord!

The line in this poem that has set most teeth on edge, and raised most blood-pressures, is the notorious one about "lesser breeds without the law" — a line which has been frequently misunderstood, for the good reason that the intended sense of it — by which the "lesser breeds" are not brown Afghans but white

Germans — is so very far from obvious. What has given less trouble, though I find it much more troublesome, is the question: *what* god of *whose* fathers? *what* lord of *whose* battle-line? The god of the German (or Russian, or Dutch Boer) battle-line is officially the Christian God, who is also — officially — the god of Mulvaney and Ortheris and Learoyd, of Tommy Atkins, "the absent-minded beggar ordered south." And so it can hardly be he to whom "Recessional" is addressed. Nor can we any more plausibly identify him as Allah or Siva or Buddha or Mithras or the god of the Parsee or the god of the Jain; although, since Kipling is fervently aware of the Indian regiments fighting beside the British in Burma and South Africa, it might reasonably seem that the God addressed should incorporate these unchristian deities at the same time as it excludes the Christian deity of Imperial Germany. How can we know where we stand, with a poem addressed to a Being so ambiguous? And yet Eliot, the devout and proudly orthodox Anglo-Catholic author of *Four Quartets,* knew just where *he* stood in respect of the poem, and where the poem stood in relation to him:

> I call Kipling a great hymn writer on the strength of *Recessional.* It is a poem almost too well known to need to have the reader's attention called to it, except to point out that it is one of the poems in which something breaks through from a deeper level than that of the mind of the conscious observer of political and social affairs — something which has the true prophetic inspiration. Kipling might have been one of the most notable of hymn writers.

This is liberal theology indeed! The Eliot whose polemics ever since "For Lancelot Andrewes" had insisted on the necessity for religious *dogma* here shows himself ready to admire a hymn that has "prophetic inspiration," though that inspiration is unleashed in the service of a Divinity undefined and undefinable. This more than makes up for Eliot's sneer at Lawrence's Congregationalism, in the sense that it overcompensates, flies to the other extreme.

Eliot had not taken leave of his senses, however. The "Lord God of hosts" of "Recessional" can indeed be identified, by just that phrase and by others in the poem that support it, particularly "Such boastings as the Gentiles use." The God addressed in "Recessional" is the God of the Old Testament, God of Israel, God of "the chosen people." If we needed supporting evidence — as in fact we don't — that evidence is in Kipling's poem of a year before, "Hymn before Action," which Eliot does not fail to print in his *Choice of Kipling's Verse* immediately before "Recessional":

> The earth is full of anger,
>   The seas are dark with wrath,
>   The Nations in their harness
>   Go up against our path:
> Ere yet we loose the legions
>   Ere yet we draw the blade,
> Jehovah of the Thunders,
>   Lord God of Battles, aid!

The God invoked in "Recessional," it now appears, is not indeed the God of Christ any more than he is the God of the Jain or the Parsee: he is the God of David, warrior king of ancient Israel.

Yet what right has Kipling, or Eliot after him, to appeal to this god, this *Yahwe*? Was Kipling, any more than Eliot, a convert to Judaism from Christianity? Quite evidently not; and so the charge of culpable frivolity lies as heavily as ever against the pair of them.

Here we may leave Eliot, remarking compassionately that in 1941 there was much excuse for a naturalized Englishman — a patriot as only the naturalized can be — to nourish the patriotic will at the expense of intellectual confusion. For Kipling there can be no such excuse. And the further we probe into Kipling's religious sentiments, the more confusion we find — and the less excuse for it.

In the 1920s his cousin Stanley Baldwin, recording how in a conversation with Kipling he had found them at one on political matters, accounted for this by saying, "We have common puritan blood." What Baldwin seems to have had in mind was that their common great-grandfather, the Scottish Ulsterman James Mac-donald, had been a Wesleyan minister converted by the great John Wesley himself. We need not deny that evangelical Wesleyanism was historically an offshoot of English puritanism. But it was a very peculiar offshoot, one that ranged itself against such great dissent-ing puritans as Oliver Cromwell and John Bunyan, with both of whom Kipling none the less aligned himself under the illusion (apparently) that in doing so he was keeping faith with his Wesleyan inheritance. Historically Wesleyanism was High Church, aggressively monarchist, Arminian, and Tory. Accordingly, if Kipling had really thought through his inheritance of Wesleyan puritanism — and *Puck of Pook's Hill* is there to show how he thought such "thinking through" was a patriotic duty — he ought to have sided with the Arminian Archbishop Laud against the Calvinist Cromwell, and with the nonjuring Arminian William Law against the Calvinist Bunyan. The Arminian conviction that Christ died for *all* men, not just for the elect, was crucial for Kipling, since it was the only basis on which for instance Gunga Din might earn salvation; and in any case the torments he suffered from his Southsea foster mother in boyhood are said to have derived from her being an evangelical Calvinist. Yet "Recessional" depends, if it is not to fall apart completely, on the Calvinist notion of a chosen people, the elect. In short, if Kipling shared his cousin Baldwin's conviction that they shared a "puritan" inheritance — and there is some reason to think that he did — he seems to have been wholly ignorant of the mutually irreconcilable strains inside English puritanism. The two logically incompatible theories of salvation, Arminian and Calvinist, are in "Recessional" held together by a powerfully traditional rhetoric; but the slightest attention to what that hymn seems to say will reveal the two incompatible systems and will break the poem in two.

Eliot decided that Kipling "can be called a Tory in a sense in which only a handful of writers together with a number of mostly inarticulate, obscure and uninfluential people are ever Tories in one generation." This enabled Eliot to clear Kipling, and also incidentally Eliot himself, from the imputation, common in 1941 and still common in England today, that the true Tory of this recondite sort is in any way friendly to fascism — the truth being rather, as Eliot says finely, that fascism, "from a truly Tory point of view, is merely the extreme degradation of democracy." Kipling certainly deserved to be rescued from this imputation, if only because of his excellent poem "The Storm Cone," in which as early as 1932 he warned against the Nazis. But as Eliot remarked further, in any less recondite sense of "Tory," anything having to do with the alignment of political parties at Westminster, Kipling was not a Tory at all. On the contrary it was the Tory party under Balfour that he assailed, savagely and bravely, in "The Islanders" (1902), with its famous and blistering indictment of "the flannelled fools at the wicket or the muddied oafs at the goals." And I think we can go further, so far as to say that Kipling believed in what has since been labeled the Whig interpretation of English history. For nothing else seems to explain his lifelong admiration of Cromwell, so much at odds with his Wesleyan inheritance and his Arminian predilections. What a strain it was for him to accommodate his Cromwellianism in the frame of his other commitments appears most strikingly from a poem that Eliot chose not to reprint, "The Old Issue," dated October 9, 1899, the date of President Kruger's ultimatum which precipitated the Boer War:

All we have of freedom, all we use or know —
This our fathers bought for us long and long ago.

Ancient Right unnoticed as the breath we draw —
Leave to live by no man's leave, underneath the Law.

Lance and torch and tumult, steel and grey-goose wing,
Wrenched it, inch and ell and all, slowly from the King.

Till our fathers 'stablished, after bloody years,
How our King is one with us, first among his peers.

So they bought us freedom — not at little cost —
Wherefore must we watch the King, lest our gain be lost.

Over all things certain, this is sure indeed,
Suffer not the old King: for we know the breed.

Give no ear to bondsmen bidding us endure,
Whining "He is weak and far"; crying "Time shall cure."

(Time himself is witness, till the battle joins,
Deeper strikes the rottenness in the people's loins.)

Give no heed to bondsmen masking war with peace.
Suffer not the old King here or overseas.

They that beg us barter — wait his yielding mood —
Pledge the years we hold in trust — pawn our brother's blood —

Howso' great their clamour, whatsoe'er their claim,
Suffer not the old King under any name!

Here is naught unproven — here is naught to learn.
It is written what shall fall if the King return.
He shall mark our goings, question whence we came,
Set his guards about us, as in Freedom's name.
He shall take a tribute; toll of all our ware;
He shall change our gold for arms — arms we may not bear.
He shall break his Judges if they cross his word;
He shall rule above the Law calling on the Lord. . . .

This has been called "complex." It is certainly complicated, and could hardly be anything else if it was to accomplish its strenuous and implausible purpose of persuading the forces of the Queen-Empress, as they advanced on the independent South African Republic, that they were in the same case as the Parliamentary armies of the 1640s advancing on the loyal armies of Charles I. The crossing over of terms in this complicated equation, so that monarchical equals parliamentarian, and republican equals despotic, is, to say the least of it, audacious. And the strenuousness of the maneuver distorts, retrospectively, the "Recessional" of two years earlier. For there the "Law" that the lesser breeds were "without" (i.e. lacking, but also "outside of") was the Law of Moses, which bore upon Israel but not on other nations; whereas in "The Old Issue" when Paul Kruger is said to "rule above the Law," the "Law" is the constitutional law of the land, and the other "Law," the Law of Moses, is presumably what the Calvinist Kruger might say he was appealing to when he was "calling on the Lord." No wonder that F. W. Reitz, Secretary of State of the South African Republic, should hurl the accusation back again:

> Gods of the Jingo — Brass and Gold,
> Lords of the world by "Right Divine,"
> Under whose baneful sway they hold
> Dominion over "Mine and Thine" . . .

It is certainly on the face of it more plausible to see the Divine Right of government, which Charles I claimed and the Cromwellians denied, being asserted by Queen Victoria than by President Kruger. Kipling has the rhetoric, but common sense and probability are all with Reitz.

It may well be thought that subsequent history has vindicated Kipling in his suspicions of the Afrikaner's mentality and political instincts. The pro-Boer demonstrators of 1900 — among them Kipling's aunt, Georgiana Burne-Jones — would be the anti-apartheid demonstrators of today. And it is true that Kipling foresaw the black South Africans getting a worse deal from the Afrikaners than from the British. But it's no good pretending that the welfare of the blacks carried any weight with Kipling when he called for war with the Boers; his case, as "The Old Issue" makes clear, rested solely on the penalties imposed upon English-speaking "Uitlanders" in the Orange Free State and the Transvaal. And certainly Calvinist theocratic republics have a poor record of safeguarding civil rights, ever since Calvin's own Geneva and the seventeenth-century Commonwealth of Massachusetts. But was it not just such a theocratic republic that was created in England by Cromwell and the other regicides? And were not just as many Englishmen deprived of their rights under the regicides as under the king who had been killed? "The Old Issue" is outrageous special pleading.

And yet we need not think that Kipling was insincere when he wrote it. On the contrary we have already found reason to think that what looks like duplicity is muddle and ignorance about the nature of the English so-called "puritan" tradition, muddle which — now as fifty years ago — is to be found particularly among those who, like Baldwin, boast of having "puritan blood." "Puritan" is not synonymous with "nonconformist," nor with "evangelical"; still less with "parliamentarian" or "democratic" or "Cromwellian." Of these adjectives, the only ones that fit the Wesleyan inheritance are "evangelical" and, less certainly, "puritan"; but Kipling, I suspect, thought that all the other adjectives were appropriate also. In short I believe that Angus Wilson is right when, on the last page of his *Strange Ride of Rudyard Kipling,* after considering various psychological explanations of the riddle that Kipling's life and works present us with, he decides: "I prefer if I must a social-historical description of long generations of Evangelical belief ending in post-Darwinian doubt."

The question of Kipling's sincerity comes up again as soon as we shift our attention from the Evangelical generations behind him to the post-Darwinian doubt that he lived in. And from this point of view it is "Recessional," not "The Old Issue," that looks inexcusable. Sons who conceive themselves to have no God at all, or only a God who is nebulous and featureless, have no right to call for help in battle on the God of their fathers whose features were stern and strong. Eliot, who decided Kipling was a great hymn-writer because of "Recessional," claims for him also that he was a great epigrammatist:

> Good epigrams in English are very few; and the great hymn writer is very rare. Both are extremely objective types of verse: they can and should be charged with intense feeling, but it must be a feeling that can be completely shared. They are possible to a writer so impersonal as Kipling.

The force of what Eliot seems to say here is carried in the words "objective" and "impersonal." But it is not clear what he means by either of these words; and if we look elsewhere in his criticism for enlightenment, we come across the famous essay "Tradition and the Individual Talent," which advances a theory of "the impersonal" that has been generally found unacceptable. I believe he is maintaining here that in a hymn (or an epigram) a poet who doesn't believe in the God of either the Old or the New Testament can properly write as if he did so believe, because by that pretense he can share the intensity of his feeling — a feeling not religious at all, but political and patriotic — with the mass of his countrymen who either *do* believe in such gods, or else think that they do. And when he cryptically quotes in full a difficult and memorable later poem, "The Fabulists," I think (for it is impossible to be sure) that he reads this poem as an impenitent confession by Kipling that he did indeed go to work in that way. However that may be, and whether or not that is a right reading of "The Fabulists," few readers will be ready to agree that, by making this play with "objective" and "impersonal," Eliot has cleared the author of "Recessional" from the charge of insincerity, of duplicity and double-dealing.

This is not to say that there is no way for an atheistic or agnostic poet, a poet of "post-Darwinian doubt," to draw on the themes and images of Christian belief. Many will agree that one of Kipling's nonbelieving contemporaries, Thomas Hardy, showed how this could be done, with moving propriety and sincerity. I need cite only "The Oxen":

> Christmas Eve, and twelve of the clock.
>   "Now they are all on their knees,"
> An elder said as we sat in a flock
>   By the embers in hearthside ease.
>
> We pictured the meek mild creatures where
>   They dwelt in their strawy pen,
> Nor did it occur to one of us there
>   To doubt they were kneeling then.
>
> So fair a fancy few would weave
>   In these years! Yet, I feel,
> If someone said on Christmas Eve,
>   "Come; see the oxen kneel
>
> "In the lonely barton by yonder coomb
>   Our childhood used to know,"
> I should go with him in the gloom,
>   Hoping it might be so.

"Hoping it might be so" expresses the agnostic sentiment with a purity, a plain and aching accuracy, such as we look for in vain anywhere in Kipling. And no talk of "objective" and "impersonal" can persuade us that "Recessional" in some quite different way is an equal or comparable achievement.

But this is not the only way in which a non-Christian or post-Christian poet can, with perfect sincerity, traffic in Christian affairs. For an alternative way of doing so we can turn to Kipling's "Gethsemane" (which, says Eliot the wily possum, "I do not think I understand"):

> The garden called Gethsemane
>   In Picardy it was,
> And there the people came to see
>   The English soldiers pass.
> We used to pass — we used to pass
>   Or halt, as it might be.

And ship our masks in case of gas
　　Beyond Gethsemane.

The garden called Gethsemane,
　　It held a pretty lass,
But all the time she talked to me
　　I prayed my cup might pass.
The officer sat on the chair,
　　The men lay on the grass,
And all the time we halted there
　　I prayed my cup might pass.

It didn't pass — it didn't pass —
　　I didn't pass from me.
I drank it when we met the gas
　　Beyond Gethsemane!

This is one of Kipling's greatest poems. And Eliot understood it well
enough, in the sense that he understood it to be overtly and fiercely
blasphemous. The poem furiously denies what every Christian is
required to believe — that one Being and one alone, Jesus, suffered
on behalf of humankind an agony more intense and more expiatory
than ever was, or ever would be, required of another. The Christian
may be, he *must* be, shocked and affronted by this; but he cannot
object to it, cannot deny that Kipling had the right to say it. Such
blasphemy is thoroughly plain-dealing, there is nothing devious nor
duplicitous. (Poetically of course — for "poetically" is the word
here, not "rhetorically" — the uncannily piercing moment comes
with the officer sitting on the chair, the exquisitely painful metrical
disturbance that lays a doubled trisyllabic rhythm on to the iambic
norm.) Straightforward blasphemous denial is another way for the
non-Christian poet to deal sincerely with Christianity. Closely related to this, and yet crucially different, is Kipling's use of Scripture
in two stories about the Great War, "The Madonna of the
Trenches" and "The Gardener." Angus Wilson, himself I think no
Christian, is quite right to protest that in both these cases the use of
the Scriptural text is both tasteless and redundant. In the first case,
where a sergeant's suffering for an unattainable woman is identified
with St. Paul's suffering for Christ, there is, as Wilson says, "plain
sentimentality clothed in a metaphysical authority which it does not

possess"; and in the second, better story, when the war cemetery's gardener is revealed to the Mary Magdalen figure as Christ himself, this has the surely unintended implication that no merely human compassion could have embraced her. Kipling seems to have intended to be blasphemous far more often than he succeeded in being so: this was because he had an uncertain grasp of what blasphemy is. That didn't in the least diminish his appeal to an exceptionally wide public; for in a post-Darwinian, post-Christian or at best nominally Christian culture, people have an uncertain grasp of blasphemy to just the extent that they have an imperfect grasp of faith. Once again, in this matter of blasphemy, it seems we can acquit Kipling of duplicity and insincerity, and convict him rather of muddle — a remarkably *fruitful* muddle, because it was a muddle that he shared with his readers, and not just with readers from the educated elite that provided other writers of his time, such as Hardy, with a far more limited public than Kipling could appeal to.

Could this be our compassionate if somewhat contemptuous verdict on Kipling's writings as a whole? I think not. "Recessional" is still the sticking point. To see in that poem no duplicity but only confusion we have to strain every nerve and give Kipling the benefit of every doubt. Moreover in Eliot's *A Choice of Kipling's Verse* there are two more poems which, if they are set side by side, raise once again in a very acute form our suspicions about Kipling's good faith. These two poems go together because they both deal with another heroic figure from the English puritan past—not Cromwell, but Bunyan. They are "The Holy War" of 1917, and "MacDonough's Song," which may have been written about 1907, though it did not appear until *A Diversity of Creatures*, in 1912. "The Holy War" is distressing rant, and it's astonishing that Eliot should have chosen it for his selection:

> All enemy divisions,
>   Recruits of every class,
> And highly screened positions
>   For flame or poison-gas;
> The craft that we call modern,
>   The crimes that we call new,

John Bunyan had 'em typed and filed
　　In Sixteen Eighty-two.
Likewise the Lords of Looseness
　　That hamper faith and works,
The Perseverance-Doubters
　　And Present-Comfort shirks,
With brittle intellectuals
　　Who crack beneath a strain —
John Bunyan met that helpful set
　　In Charles the Second's reign.

Emmanuel's vanguard dying
　　For right and not for rights,
My Lord Apollyon lying
　　To the State-kept Stockholmites,
The Pope, the swithering Neutrals,
　　The Kaiser and his Gott —
Their rôles, their goals, their naked souls —
　　He knew and drew the lot.

The earlier poem is much more distinguished writing, and just for that reason it is, especially at the end (which I shall not quote), even more shocking. But what rocks us on our heels is that Bunyan's very phrase, "The Holy War," which in 1917 is endorsed and applauded, had those several years before been treated with searing contempt:

Whether the State can loose and bind
　　In Heaven as well as on Earth:
If it be wiser to kill mankind
　　Before or after the birth —
These are matters of high concern
　　Where State-kept schoolmen are;
But Holy State (we have lived to learn)
　　Endeth in Holy War.

(Just so; but Holy War against the Boers was precisely what Kipling had preached in "The Old Issue"!) "MacDonough's Song" is part and parcel of a story, "As Easy as A.B.C.," which is set in the year 2065 A.D. And so we may say — it seems we *must* say — that Holy War will be manifestly a vicious and desolating idea in 2065, though it is a wholesome and invigorating idea in 1917. But this implies a relativism — about art and morals and politics, indeed about *truth* — for which the only word is "cynical." And if this is what "puritanism" brings us to, as soon as it is conceived of as a secular and time-bound entity persisting apart from religious faith, then "puritan blood" is what no one can or should take pride in. One does not have to be a knee-jerk liberal, nor one of the "brittle intellectuals," to believe that the Kipling who thought this and perverted his poetic vocation to serve this kind of thinking, is indeed in many ways the diabolical figure that many of us supposed him to be, before Eliot and George Orwell some forty years ago began to rehabilitate him.

Note

1. Under the title, "A Puritan's Empire: The Case of Kipling," this essay first appeared in *The Sewanee Review* 87, no. 1 (Winter 1979), pp. 34–48.

Dissent and Individualism[1]

If we open a recent survey of British and American poetry since 1939[2], we are introduced in the second sentence to the poet Louis MacNeice:

> The son of the man who became Anglican Bishop of Down, Connor and Dromore, educated at Marlborough and Oxford, a classics don at the University of Birmingham, and a producer and scriptwriter in the B.B.C.: the biography is less that of an individual and more like that of his class.

It had perhaps not occurred to us that just four items of a personal history, strung together, could be called "a biography." But if we can agree to that, and can concede for instance that if James Boswell had had our advantages he could with profit have boiled down his Life of Johnson into far more manageable compass (say, two sides of a sheet of paper), we shall be that much nearer understanding how a class — that is to say, a conceptual category, a notion, a mental convenience — can nowadays be accorded life, the sort of "Life" indeed that a more streamlined modern Boswell may be called on to write. In fact of course if the individuals Louis MacNeice and Samuel Johnson can be seen most truly as instances of a category, a *class*, then the modern Boswell would be a fool if he portrayed the individuals rather than the class which comprehends them. And only the dilettante will tremble at what may happen, under this dispensation, to those individuals that we call *poems*, which are as tender and sometimes almost as intricate as the human individuals that we call "persons." Rough justice indeed is the best they can hope for, poems and people alike — as this survey soon shows.

Proceeding in this way is sometimes called, and sometimes calls itself, "Marxist." But it has ancestors far more remote, and far less reputable, than Karl Marx. One time in England when individuals were thus confidently categorized, judged, and in some measure proscribed — all on the basis of three or four facts about their birth, education, religious allegiance, and occupation — was the late seventeenth century. Among the true ancestors of our modern classifiers were the vengeful members of parliament under Charles II who thus categorized and proscribed the English Nonconformists. When the penal proscription was lifted and religious toleration in large measure secured, the Nonconformists properly saw this as a triumph for the individual against the facile classifiers and categorizers who had decided all Dissenters were traitors to the State:

If Christians be first denominated by general titles and terms of distinction, which they cannot help, and then the crimes of any particular person, that the world pleases to denominate as one of the same party, must be charged and imputed to the whole; what must the consequence of this be, but that the whole community become obnoxious to punishment, and the very government itself thereupon be dissolved?

For I take it to be past denial or doubt, that some of each denomination have been, are, or may be guilty of seditious practices. Some hypocrites will lurk among those vast bodies of people, under the most strict and watchful government; but God forbid their guilt should affect the whole body, under whose names they shelter themselves. God, reason, and conscience, do all command the hottest zeal, to make its pause and just distinction here. Let the guilty be brought to condign punishment, upon fair trial and conviction. This discourse designs no favour for such. But let not those who abhor their wickedness, and are as pure from their crimes as yourselves, suffer with them or for them: For then your reason will tell you, yourselves are as liable to sufferings as they; and that your zeal is not kindled by love to justice, but the hatred of a party.

It is not in the body politic, as in the body natural: If the hand steal, the feet are justly laid in irons, and the neck put into an halter; because all the members of the body natural are animated, and governed but by one soul. But in the body politic, every individual hath a distinct soul of his own; and therefore that member only that offends ought to be punished, and all the rest to enjoy their full liberty and honour as before. Away therefore for ever with this church and state destroying synechdoche.[3]

"Synecdoche," says the dictionary: "a figure" (that is to say, in rhetoric) "by which a more comprehensive term is used for a less comprehensive or vice versa; as whole for part or part for whole, genus for species or species for genus, etc." And this is individualism too: John Flavel in the 1690s would risk pedantry for the sake of wit; he had a powerful and learned mind, he would not conceal the fact, and it seems that his fellow-Dissenters, less well endowed or lacking his educational advantages, took vicarious pride in his performance. A hundred years later a dissenting minister would hardly have taken the risk, and for *his* successor, now in the 1970s, it would be unthinkable; it would give too much offense, for it would be thought (under our tyranny of the majority) *elitist*, "undemocratic." But then John Flavel differs from later Dissenters in all sorts of ways; in his mouth, for instance, the locution "church and state" has no harshly jeering inflection. The Dissenters, we like to say, vindicated the rights of the individual against the state; but this is true only if we assume that the state is in the hands of, or at the mercy of, the inveterate and facile classifiers. And Flavel seems to assume that this doesn't have to be so; he might have argued, as certainly *we* may argue, that precisely the Crown — the monarch, who is above all classifications — has a constitutional duty to see that this doesn't happen.

More generally, however, are we not laboring the obvious? That there is a close tie between religious Dissent and individualism is what no one will deny. Very well. But in that case how does a Dissenter respond, when he returns to the account of Louis MacNeice? There he reads, of "the dilemma MacNeice faced in the 1940s":

He cannot praise the world too keenly, for the socialist in him knows that it is rotten, unjust and dying. But neither can he condemn it unequivocally. The ambivalent values of the bourgeoisie leave room for manoeuvre, for the flowering of an individualism which, though it may be historically finished, defines the essence of our (bourgeois) notions of humanity.

A Dissenter, or any Christian for that matter, may well wonder in the first place why a son of the Bishop of Dromore had to wait for socialism to tell him that the world "is rotten, unjust and dying." For this is what every Christian knows, as John Flavel certainly knew it, without any socialism to tell him so. The Christian knows also that, unjust and corrupt as the world is, he cannot "condemn it unequivocally"; indeed, he goes further, for he knows that any attempt thus to condemn it is a *sin* — against God, who created this world, unsatisfactory as it is or has become.

Oh but (it will be said) this is to fly too high — in the passage we are looking at, "the world" does not mean *the world*. It does not include for instance the natural creation; the writer does not mean to impugn lambs or tigers, deserts or mountains. Indeed, his world that is called "rotten, unjust and dying" does not comprehend, necessarily or even probably, Tanzanian or Eskimo, Albanian or Chinese; his use of the word "bourgeois" shows clearly on the contrary, for those who will read him with candor, that by "world" he means only that manmade social fabric which Louis MacNeice had to contend with — the United Kingdom and the United States in the 1940s. Summoning our candor to stifle, as best we can, uncharitable wishes that people would say what they mean, and would curb their addiction to synecdoche ("by which a more comprehensive term is used for a less comprehensive"), also passing by for the moment this revelation that a Christian's sense of the injustice in the world is a great deal more thoroughgoing than a socialist's, let us try to engage with our author on the basis of what he meant to say, rather than what he said. Even so, I'm afraid, our difficulties are not over. For even after we have agreed to take "world" to mean only that human creation, the society that MacNeice moved in through the 1930s into the 1940s, we find ourselves stumbling over the assumption that this world was indeed "human," manmade. John Flavel did not think so. In his Coronation sermon, preached at Dartmouth, he declared:

> When God puts a crown upon the head, and a sceptre into the hand
> of a man, he engraves upon that man (in a qualified sense) both his
> name, and the lively characters of his Majesty and authority. . . . But
> yet, in all the grants and conveyances of Heaven, there is always a
> reservation and salvo to the divine prerogative, to displace at plea-
> sure, and set it upon what head he shall please. . . .[4]

Whereas to the Unitarian Richard Price in 1790 it seemed clear that
the People had the right to "cashier" a monarch who had mis-
behaved, to the Presbyterian John Flavel in 1691 it seemed clear that
only God had that right; and if it be objected that it is hard to
discern God's purposes at such junctures, one retorts that, as recorded history has shown, it is no less hard to discern the purposes
of that amorphous and convenient entity, "the people."

Since we are trying to find a common ground on which dispute
can be profitable, can we leave that momentous question in
abeyance, and agree to proceed on the assumption that British
society, as MacNeice the Anglo-Irishman experienced it in the
1930s and 1940s, was indeed wholly a manmade contrivance? I'm
not sure that we can do this, or that we should. For if God did not
participate in the making of British society, he at all events permitted it to be made. If he exists, there is no equation that he can be
left out of. And I suspect that it is our civil concessions to our
secular antagonists "for the sake of argument," that have bedevilled
and disabled the Christian witness in these matters.

However, if against our better judgments we take this risky
maneuver and agree to read our commentator in an artificially
secular spirit, we discover I think that what we call "the Christian,"
he calls "the bourgeois." For the Christian, as we have seen, is
required to be ambivalent: he must dispise and reject "the world"
at the same time as he loves and respects it. And for our commentator it is the values of the "bourgeoisie" that are "ambivalent." The
implication is that the values of other orders of society are free of
this ambivalence. (And this is our commentator's implication, not
ours; *we* may be very willing to think that this, as we think, necessary and proper ambivalence is to be found in proletariat and
aristocracy — it is he who restricts this Christian sentiment to the
one class that he calls the *bourgeoisie*).

One thing, at least, is quite clear, and enough to take our breath away. If, as is generally conceded, our Dissenting forebears suffered and sometimes died for "individualism," that individualism is — we are asked to think — "historically finished." At this point we mount into metaphysics. For, "historically finished" though it is, this individualism can still, it appears, "flower." And this can only mean that by "history" and "historical" our commentator does not mean what common sense means by those words. In his discourse "History" is as much a transcendent and immanent force as "God" is in ours. And it is this divinity, not ours, that has — we are asked to think — shoveled individualism into a dustbin whence it can, however, unaccountably "flower."

But of course one sees clearly enough what our commentator is driving at, and why right-thinking people are, if not persuaded by him, at least disturbed. "Individualism" smells much less sweetly in the nostrils when we join it with the word "economic." "*Economic* individualism" — it is this baleful conjuction that has long given to Dissenters a special place in the demonology of the British Left, as when E. P. Thompson, on no better evidence than a novel by Frances Trollope, decides in his *Making of the English Working Class* that the hardhearted mill-owners of the 1820s were characteristically Dissenters, though the villainous overseers whom they employed were Methodists. (On the other hand, confusingly, Dissenters as the heirs of Cromwellian republicanism also appear in leftist mythology on the side of the angels.) John Flavel did not foresee — how could he? — the advent of Adam Smith or of industrial capitalism. If he had lived to see it, there is no need to suppose that his loyalty to individualism would have led him to deplore state intervention to prevent, for instance, unemployment. Quite the contrary:

> It is therefore the undoubted interest of Christian states and churches, to make every individual person as useful as may be to the whole, and to enjoy the services of all their subjects and members, one way or another, according to their different capacities; that it may be said of them (as the historian speaks of the land of Canaan) that there was in it, *Nihil infructuosum, nihil sterile*; not a shrub but bare some fruit.

There is nothing in the Dissenting tradition which sets its face against state intervention to ensure an acceptable measure of economic equality and security; though equally there is nothing there to solve the riddle which confronts us today: how to ensure this measure of equality without at the same time curtailing political liberty, how to restrain economic individualism while not curbing and stunting political and cultural and religious individualism. And plainly, it is these — not merely economic individualism — that our commentator has in his sights, when he speaks of "an individualism which, though it may be historically finished, defines the essence of our (bourgeois) notions of humanity." Here too, try as I may, I can assign no meaning to "bourgeois" except "Christian." How this may be will become a little clearer if we ask what alternative is offered for our approval in place of the individualism supposedly discredited: what it is that History, having "finished" with that, is now engendering in its stead? To this natural question we are given no clear answer. The nearest we come is a series of locutions on a later page, still concerned with MacNeice: "true conviviality"; "the idea of community"; "the ideal of an organic community"; "the meaning of community, its power of ennobling the essentially negative work of critical diagnosis." It is hard to know what to do with such evasive and muffled expressions as these, though it is not hard to guess what it is that they are muffling, what quite clear and programmatic notions are being hidden away behind them. All one can say with certainty is that these expressions, set over against "individualism," seek to replace a series of vertical relationships — as of a man with his king, and his God — with a web of horizontal relationships, as of a man with his fellows. And fellowship is at the heart of Christianity, is it not? Well no, it is not; it may be *near* to the heart, it is not *at* the heart — or so John Flavel seems to say. For on the one hand he tells us:

> This natural quality of sociableness is diversely improved. Sometimes sinfully, in wicked combinations to do mischief; like the herding together of wolves and tygers; such was the consideration of Simeon and Levi, brethren in iniquity; Gen. XLIX. 56. Sometimes it is improved civilly, for the more orderly and prosperous management of human affairs. Thus all civilized countries have im-

proved it, for the common security and benefit. And sometimes religiously, for the better promoting of each other's spiritual and eternal good.

But elsewhere, as we have seen, he insists: "It is not in the body politic, as in the body natural: . . . in the body politic, every individual hath a distinct soul of his own; . . ." And in any case what he calls "sociableness" (which we may take as roughly equivalent to "community" or "true conviviality") is for him ethically neutral — since it can be "improved," he says, "sinfully in wicked combinations to do mischief," as well as beneficially. Fellowship may be a grace of the religious life, a happy consequence of it, an invaluable aid to the attaining and sustaining of it, but it cannot be the *end* of that life, the main or sufficient thing to be aimed at. And so, however expressions like "community" or "true conviviality" may strike an answering chord in a Christian breast — that of course is their rhetorical function—they are profoundly unchristian if they are offered in place of individualism, of "every individual hath a distinct soul of his own." No form of Christianity can afford to make that switch, and Dissenting Christianity least of all.

One may go further and suggest that "community" is an ignoble end to aim at, not just in religion but even in politics. Even if we did not know what it means in practice — that is to say, a central and swollen bureaucracy trying to impose equality at the level of the lowest common denominator — and even if we did not know from experience that it is inherently inefficient and cannot compass the ends it aims at, what sort of an ideal is it anyway, for private and public life to be bent towards? An undiscriminating and unrestricted "togetherness," as of cows huddled together in a byre to keep one another warm, one cosy and hearty *steam* enveloping the entire citizenry, a vocabulary in which "ordinary" and "common" are the terms of highest praise and greatest warmth, in which "human" and "social" are interchangeable — is *that* what the less than utopian hopes of a Burke, a Montesquieu, or a John Adams have come down to, as the utmost to which a commonwealth may aspire? Undoubtedly it is *one* way (though foredoomed to failure, incidentally) of ridding ourselves of classes and classifiers; John Flavel saw another way, and a better one.

Flavel's way is not the way of the Church, as that was understood for instance by T. S. Eliot; it is the way of Christ, who speaks to every individual's "distinct soul of his own," and is recognized there, or else is not recognized at all. Having achieved this recognition, we may come to recognize what it means to say that our secular affairs are all "in the hand of God." We must not think that God *willed* Britain to sink to its present ignoble condition. But we must think that he is aware of it, that he feels for us in it, and that he is working out his purposes through it. We may have in mind how in our own day a disconcerting Huguenot historian, Jacques Ellul, reflects upon Samaria, the Northern Kingdom of Israel, under siege from the Syrians (the second Book of Kings):

> Why this distress? Israel is no worse than other peoples. It is no worse at this moment in its history than at other moments. There is no reason, motive, cause, or condition for God's free will. God is God. He speaks, and things are. We have not to think that behind there might be something different. This unhappy people is again led into even greater evil by the trial itself. Under the suffering of the siege it does not prove to be heroic or virtuous. On the contrary, crime and oppression increase. . . . Conversely, there is no reason why the trial should cease. There is no comprehensible motive for God's arresting of the situation and raising of the siege. . . . He chooses the moment of deliverance, too, in absolute freedom. . . . One day the Word of God will break over man and declare: "Lo, the trial is over." This moment is God's secret.[5]

It is part of our ignoble estimation of ourselves that we suppose this language, and this scriptural analogue, altogether too lofty to fit our condition, so humorously have we domesticated *our* "trial," *our* long siege. But it's precisely this — our ignobility in our own eyes, our pride and pleasure in being "ordinary," our determination to see ourselves and our fellow-citizens as manikins rather than men and women — that prevents us from taking the measure of the condition we have sunk to, and from finding any hope in it. One symptom of that is our tamely submitting to the classifiers who tell us that our dignity and significance reside in our belonging to this class or that one, not in being individuals, each with a soul to save or not to save, as severally we (and no one else) may decide.

One poet of our time — no Calvinist, and as it happens not an English-speaker — had anticipated Jacques Ellul's declaration: "God is God. He speaks and things are." This poet had divined not just the meaning of this, and the necessary truth of it, but the paradoxical consolation wrapped within it. He was Boris Pasternak, speaking through the mouth of his own fiction, Dr. Yuri Zhivago, and meditating on that most disconcerting of Christ's miracles, his blasting of the barren fig-tree:

> Had leaf and branch and root and stem been granted
> One moment's freedom, then the laws of Nature
> Had made all haste, and doom been intercepted.
> But a miracle is a miracle, a miracle is God.
> When we are all at odds it comes upon us
> Instantaneous, and when least expected.

Notes

1. This essay first appeared in *Proteus* No. 1 (November, 1977) pp. 22 — 30.
2. Eric Homberger, *The Art of the Real: Poetry in England and America since 1939* (1977).
3. John Flavel (1630?— 1691). *The Reasonableness of Personal Reformation* (1691). *The Works of John Flavel* (1820, reprinted 1968, London), Vol. VI.
4. Ibid.
5. Jacques Ellul, *Politique de Dieu, politiques de l'homme* (Paris, 1966); translated by G. W. Bromiley as *The Politics of God and the Politics of Man* (1972), pp. 57 — 8.

Index of Names